T0315862

KEY IDEAS IN TORT LAW

This book offers nine key ideas about tort law that will help the reader to understand its various social functions and evaluate its effectiveness in performing those functions. The book focuses, in particular, on how tort law can guide people's behaviour, and the political and social environments within which it operates. It also provides the reader with a wealth of detail about the ideas and values that underlie tort 'doctrine'—tort law's rules and principles, and the way those rules and principles operate in practice. The book is an accessible introduction to tort law that will provide students, scholars and practitioners alike with a fresh and engaging view of the subject.

Key Ideas in Law: Volume 2

Key Ideas in Law

Series Editor: Nicholas J McBride

Hart Publishing's series *Key Ideas in Law* offers short, stimulating introductions to legal subjects, providing an opportunity to step back from the detail of the law to consider its broader intellectual foundations and ideas, and how these work in practice.

Written by leading legal scholars with great expertise and depth of knowledge, these books offer an unparalleled combination of accessibility, concision, intellectual breadth and originality in legal writing.

Each volume will appeal to students seeking a concise introduction to a subject, stimulating wider reading for a course or deeper understanding for an exam, as well as to scholars and practitioners for the fresh perspectives and new ideas they provide.

Recent titles in this series:

For the complete list of titles in this series, see 'Key Ideas in Law' link at www.bloomsburyprofessional.com/uk/series/key-ideas-in-law/

Key Ideas in Tort Law

Peter Cane

·HART·
PUBLISHING
OXFORD AND PORTLAND, OREGON
2017

Hart Publishing

An imprint of Bloomsbury Publishing Plc

Hart Publishing Ltd
Kemp House
Chawley Park
Cumnor Hill
Oxford OX2 9PH
UK

Bloomsbury Publishing Plc
50 Bedford Square
London
WC1B 3DP
UK

www.hartpub.co.uk
www.bloomsbury.com

Published in North America (US and Canada) by
Hart Publishing
c/o International Specialized Book Services
920 NE 58th Avenue, Suite 300
Portland, OR 97213-3786
USA

www.isbs.com

HART PUBLISHING, the Hart/Stag logo, BLOOMSBURY and the
Diana logo are trademarks of Bloomsbury Publishing Plc

First published 2017

British Library Cataloguing-in-Publication Data

A catalogue record for this book is available from the British Library.

ISBN:	PB:	978-1-50990-942-1
	ePDF:	978-1-50990-944-5
	ePub:	978-1-50990-943-8

Library of Congress Cataloging-in-Publication Data

Names: Cane, Peter, 1950- author.

Title: Key ideas in tort law / Peter Cane.

Description: Oxford [UK] ; Portland, Oregon : Hart Publishing, 2017. |
Series: Key ideas in law ; vol. 2 | Includes bibliographical references and index.

Identifiers: LCCN 2017029129 (print) | LCCN 2017030103 (ebook) |
ISBN 9781509909438 (Epub) | ISBN 9781509909421 (pbk. : alk. paper)

Subjects: LCSH: Torts—England. | Torts.

Classification: LCC KD1949 (ebook) | LCC KD1949 .C36 2017 (print) | DDC 346.4203—dc23

LC record available at https://lccn.loc.gov/2017029129

Typeset by Compuscript Ltd, Shannon

To find out more about our authors and books visit www.hartpublishing.co.uk. Here you will find extracts,
author information, details of forthcoming events and the option to sign up for our newsletters.

For Jane,
who has taught me much of what I know about tort law

CONTENTS

1

Nine Key Ideas

This book is about tort law—English tort law, to be more precise. Laws come in 'legal systems', and legal systems are traditionally associated with political communities. For instance, Scotland has (and has always had) its own legal system, as do the USA, Australia, China and so on. Laws differ to a greater or lesser extent from one system to another. For instance, US tort law is significantly different in many ways from English tort law, which is very different from Chinese tort law, reflecting the fact that the USA, England and China are different political communities and have different cultures. We might say that this book is about 'one of many tort laws'.

It is addressed primarily to readers who know something about law in general, and tort law in particular, but who find what they do know puzzling, or simply want to know more. The book presents nine 'key ideas' about tort law:

KI 1 Tort law is law.

KI 2 Tort law is the law of torts.

KI 3 Each tort has two main elements: (1) conduct that is classified by tort law as wrongful and (2) one or more interests with which that conduct has interfered in ways specified by tort law.

KI 4 Torts are only one species of legal wrongs.

KI 5 Tort law is rarely enforced.

KI 6 Tort law is political.

KI 7 Tort law 'has its uses'.

KI 8 Tort law is not 'the only game in town'.

KI 9 Tort law is here to stay—live with it!

I expect that you will find at least some of these ideas paradoxical, if not downright weird. I hope that this will spark your interest in reading further because each of these ideas hints at important truths about tort law. They will not all receive the same amount of development, if only because some of them raise profoundly complex and difficult issues that cannot be fully explored in a book such as this. The overall aim is to provide background to what is sometimes called 'legal doctrine' and to breathe life into the sometimes rather bloodless words on the pages of tort books.

It is worth reflecting for a minute on this word 'doctrine', which might strike you as a rather odd one to use. Surely the contents of tort books are not to be compared to the contents of sacred texts such as the Christian Bible or the Muslim Koran? In fact, however, law and religion share at least one basic characteristic: both are based on authority. Just as sacred texts are invested with the authority of some holy person or supernatural God, so legal texts are invested with the authority of the legal officials and institutions that make them—notably, legislatures and courts. Devout Christians and Muslims invest their sacred texts with the authority of God and treat the contents as 'God's word'. In a somewhat similar way, 'law-abiding' people, who 'take law seriously', treat what its makers have said—'the law'—as authoritative. Law, we might say, requires 'a leap of faith' (Gardner 2012a).* Legal officials who implement and enforce the law must take it seriously in this way, at least when they are performing their official functions. Whatever they may actually think about the law, if law is to operate as it is meant to, they must behave as if they were true believers. However, law students and legal scholars as such do not have official responsibilities of this sort, and they are free (and may be thought to have an obligation) to stand back from the law and treat it not (only) as an authoritative regime of rules but (also) as an object of dispassionate study in much the same way as historians and sociologists of religion study the beliefs and behaviour of Christians, Muslims and so on.

The key ideas presented in this book could be summed up in **One Really Big Idea** (the **ORBI**) that (tort) law is an authority-based phenomenon that can be, and is best, understood both 'from the inside' as an authoritative source of guidance about how to behave and also 'from the outside', taking into account tort law's character as law, the political and social environments in which tort law operates, tort law's uses, and its

---

* Throughout this book, full references to books and articles referenced in the text can be found by consulting the Bibliography at the back of the book.

competitors. From this 'external' perspective, authoritative legal doctrine is only one aspect of tort law's social nature. It is law's authority that enables it to perform the social functions we can use it fulfil. Understanding the doctrine is important, but so is appreciating the environments and contexts in which the doctrine is embedded and in which it comes to life off the page. Understanding (tort) law in all its doctrinal and social richness and diversity teaches us something about the 'human condition', about what it means to be human. The hope is that this book will encourage readers to begin that exciting, life-long task of discovery.

2

Tort Law

KI 1: Tort law is law

How, you will immediately protest, can such a tautologous banality teach us anything about tort law, let alone about 'the human condition'? A simple, but adequate, answer is that philosophers and lawyers have argued for millennia—and still argue vigorously today—about what law is. Law is such a complex and sprawling social phenomenon that providing a convincing account of its nature is a very tall order indeed; and various different accounts compete with one another for acceptance. Since tort law is (by definition) an aspect of the larger body of 'the law', it is useful to begin by focusing our attention on the whole rather than on the particular part.

Law, in the sense we are thinking about it in this book, is a product of human social life and interaction. It is, we might say, a 'human social practice' and an aspect of a society's 'culture'. We do not know when, in the course of human history, this social practice first appeared; but we can be confident that the human species has existed for much longer than what we are calling 'law'. It has been speculated that law appears only when human social groups reach a certain size, and their activities a certain level of complexity.

Law is a social practice of a particular sort that we might call 'normative'. At its core, what this means is that law is about how human beings living in societies should behave towards one another—what they may, ought and ought not to do; what is permitted, required and prohibited in our dealings with one another. Besides law, another very important normative, social practice is morality. Like law, the nature of morality has been a subject of intense debate for thousands of years, as has the nature of the relationship between law and morality. Therefore, what I say here on these (as on many other) topics should be treated as a point of view, not 'the truth' in any absolute or unquestionable sense. As a first thought, you might suppose that law and morality are obviously very different things. In fact, it turns out to be quite difficult to distinguish one from the other.

Law is a social practice in at least two distinct senses: first, it is made by humans; and secondly, it is an aspect of social life. As for the first, many people think that morality is not 'made' by humans. Some believe that it is made 'by God', while others believe that 'true morality' is not made by anyone and, like the natural world, exists independently of human activity. A good reason to take one or the other of these two views is that one of the uses of morality in our lives is to supply a set of 'norms' to which individuals are personally committed, and which they can use as a benchmark against which to assess the validity and legitimacy of demands made on them by other individuals and by society as a whole. Morality, if you like, provides individuals with a shield against what they consider to be unreasonable external pressure to behave in certain ways and not others. It is, at least, comforting to think that such 'personal morality' consists not merely of one's own, perhaps idiosyncratic, views about what one may do, and ought or ought not to do, but that they are, in some sense, valid and binding for everyone. After all, unless you think that the norms you personally subscribe to are objectively correct in some sense, what right do you have to complain when other people demand that you act inconsistently with one of those norms or, conversely, to expect others to comply with them?

For present purposes, it is not necessary to answer this question because all we need to say to distinguish morality from law is that personal morality may be used as an ultimate standard against which to assess and judge the acceptability of law. Put differently, personal morality provides individuals with norms that they believe they themselves should conform to and, more importantly, that everyone else as well should conform to, regardless of what the law says. If you thought that you alone were required to conform to a particular norm, you might not think of that norm as 'moral'.

The second sense in which law is a social practice is that it is an aspect of social life. In this sense, morality, too, is a social practice. Philosophers sometimes say that morality tells us 'what we owe to each other' (Scanlon 1998). We may distinguish between personal morality, in the sense explained in the previous paragraph, and 'social morality'. One way of thinking about social morality is that it is 'made' by society; but it is probably more helpful to understand it more vaguely as reflecting some sort of 'moral consensus amongst right-thinking people'. So, for instance, we may say that 'community morality' in England condemns the death penalty as a criminal punishment, but that community morality in the United States is seriously polarised on this issue. Social morality is not so much about 'what we owe to each other' but rather 'what individuals owe to society'. Like personal morality, morality in this social sense can provide a benchmark against which to test the validity and legitimacy of the law. In that guise, morality has two main uses. First, it can be used by the powerful in society—the 'establishment', the 'government'—to support the validity and legitimacy of legal demands made upon its members in the name of 'society'. Second, by contrast, it may be used to resist legal demands made in society's name on the ground that in making those demands, the law (and those who support it) are in conflict with community morality.

It should be clear from this that social morality and personal morality may be in conflict: personal morality may be used to assess and criticise social morality as much as to assess and criticise law. We might say that personal and social morality play different roles in people's lives: personal morality can be used to protect individuals' 'personal identities' while social morality can be deployed to protect their 'social identities'.

So far, we have not made much progress in distinguishing between law and morality. Some people think that unlike law, morality is not 'made'; but not everyone agrees. Law, personal morality and social morality are all normative social phenomena in the sense that they are concerned primarily with the ways we may, should or should not interact with other individuals, and with social groups and our society as a whole. However, one respect in which law does differ quite clearly from morality (whether personal or social) is that law is more 'institutionalised' than morality; and this difference has very significant practical consequences. Law is made by legislatures ('Parliament') and courts; it is implemented by officials and agencies of the executive branch of government; observance of the law is monitored by various officials and bodies with 'policing' responsibilities; and it is applied and enforced by tribunals and courts. Legislatures, executives, police, courts and tribunals, bailiffs and sheriffs, are the archetypal legal institutions. This is not to say that there are no 'moral institutions'. For instance, morality that is based on an organised religion may well be made, implemented, policed, applied and enforced (in part, anyway) by religious officials and bodies—religious 'authorities'.

Also, parents, carers and guardians may function as moral officials in dealing with those under their control or with whose well-being they are charged. In general, however, such institutions play little or no part in the moral lives of autonomous adults. For most people, most of the time, there are no moral legislatures, moral police or moral courts. For instance, to say that someone is 'acting like moral police' is typically a form of criticism, not approval.

Because law is underpinned and supported by an elaborate institutional framework it can be used for purposes that morality is not able to promote as well, or at all. Because morality is typically not the product of deliberate human activity but emerges, develops and changes gradually and organically, its requirements tend to be too abstract and general to provide detailed guidance about right and good behaviour. For instance, a common—indeed, a probably universal—moral principle prohibits harming other people by behaving unsafely. Exceeding the speed limit when driving can be unsafe and risks harm to others as well as oneself. Therefore, the general moral injunction against causing harm by unsafe conduct applies to creating risks of harm by speeding. But what amounts to speeding? Most people's morality would probably not provide a specific answer to this question. Rather, we look to the law for the answer—say 30 mph here, 40 mph there and 50 mph somewhere else. These are speeds that society, through its authoritative law-makers, have declared to be generally safe in the various locations to which they apply. Provided the law's answers to such questions are consistent with the general moral principle they relate to, they become (as it were) part of morality. Law can supplement morality in this way because it has law-making institutions that can generate answers to moral questions in a way that morality cannot do (or, at least, not so efficiently and effectively). Morality, we might say, 'depends on law' (Honoré 1993). From this perspective, law is morality made determinate.

Take the example of taxation. Most peoples' moral compass points them in the direction of supporting social life by paying taxes; and it may even identify general principles such as: 'from each according to their means'—the basic idea underlying the concept of 'progressive taxation'. But morality is unlikely to tell anyone how much to pay. It is the law that can and does do that. This example also suggests that legal supplements to morality may become so grafted onto the host that a person might feel able to criticise tax law *on moral grounds* for requiring them to pay too much. Putting the point generally, by virtue of its complex institutionalisation, law can give us answers to 'moral' questions that morality, by itself, cannot generate. An important constraint on law's ability to do this is that the answers it provides must be consistent with the rest of a person's morality if that person is to feel a legally-derived moral obligation to conform to the law's requirements. Morality needs law, but law is subject to morality.

Rules of the road also illustrate another way in which law's institutional resources enable it to supplement morality. The moral imperative not to harm others by unsafe conduct requires us all to drive on the same side of the road; but the decision whether to drive on the right or the left is, we might say, morally neutral—provided a decision is made one way or the other, morality is satisfied regardless of which side is chosen. Philosophers refer to this sort of decision as being concerned purely with 'coordination' of human behaviour. By contrast, for instance the choice between various possible speed limits is much more than a matter of coordination: it is not enough that everyone is required to drive at the same speed—that speed must also promote safety. People are unlikely to disagree 'on moral grounds' about which side of the road to drive on; but they may well disagree about the safe speed to drive at.

With this general discussion under our belts, let's return to tort law. On the one hand, tort law, like law generally, is subject to moral evaluation. Because law and morality are both social normative practices, they cover much the same ground as one another. In some cases, morality and law may contain one and the same norm—for instance, do not deliberately cause another person physical injury unless you have some justification for doing so. In fact, many legal norms simply reflect more-or-less identical moral norms. If this were not so, the law would be open to pervasive and constant criticism for being inconsistent with morality. Stable and successful social life depends on law being largely congruent with the morality of the bulk of society's members (Goodin 2010). We might speculate that people who know what the law requires will be more inclined to conform to it if it is consistent with their personal morality. Anyway, most people know little law. Such people, we might suppose, will be much more likely to conform to the law if what the law tells them to do is what their morality would require of them independently of the law. Many of the more general principles of tort law, as well as its more detailed rules, would strike most people as being 'moral common-sense' either because they more-or-less precisely reproduce moral principles or, especially in the case of more detailed rules that supplement such principles, the rules are consistent with those principles. This is not to say that tort law raises no morally controversial issues. For instance, there has been considerable debate about 'the morality' of awarding damages against a doctor whose negligence in performing a sterilisation operation leads to the birth of an unwanted but healthy child (Cane 2004); and of compensating the so-called 'worried well'—people who have, for instance, been tortiously exposed to a potentially harmful substance such as asbestos without, so far, suffering any physical harm, but who worry that one day they will succumb to some asbestos-related disease, such as asbestosis, or lung cancer or mesothelioma, as a result of their exposure, and who seek recompense for the anxiety of knowing that one day they may become ill.

Such examples alert us to several other things that law can do by virtue of having the sort of institutional support that morality typically lacks. One is to manage moral disagreement. Members of modern societies disagree about all sorts of moral issues that affect their dealings with others. In some—perhaps many—cases, we can live perfectly happily together while 'agreeing to disagree'. In other cases of disagreement, however, allowing people to follow their own personal morality regardless of what others think and do may produce social conflict and instability, and may even lead to violence. In the US, pervasive disagreement over the moral status of abortion regularly leads not only to social conflict but even to criminal behaviour such as murder and arson. Law can play an important role in preventing disagreement over ideas and values turning into dysfunctional behaviour. It is law's authoritativeness that enables it to perform this function. People who accept that the law has authority over them may be prepared to comply with it even if it is inconsistent with their personal morality, provided that they believe this will promote beneficial social harmony. Of course, if people do not respect the law, or the law is inconsistent with some moral principle that they consider to be fundamentally important and, in some sense, non-negotiable, they may not be prepared to comply even if this would promote harmony. For them, the personal moral cost of compliance for the sake of social harmony would be too high. It is, perhaps, not easy to think of rules or principles of tort law that would raise such strong feelings: we will likely feel able to live even with those aspects of tort law with which we disagree on moral grounds in the knowledge that others, with whom we value living in social harmony, think differently.

Another area in which law's institutional resources give it an edge over morality is that of detecting and investigating wrongs and providing remedies. Because, for most people, there are no moral police or courts, there is no one that victims of moral wrongs can call upon to help them bring to light and investigate such wrongs. As for remedies, because of the institutional weakness of morality, many moral penalties, punishments and redress typically take forms that do not require the alleged wrongdoer to do anything very demanding. By contrast, because decisions of legal institutions are backed by the state's legitimate power of coercion, they can effectively impose a wide variety of punishments and remedies on wrongdoers, including the payment of compensation, which is the most common remedy for torts.

We may summarise the discussion in this chapter by saying that because tort rules and principles are law, they are backed up by law's institutional resources. The significance of this point for our purposes is that the powers and capacities of legal institutions make a major contribution to lifting tort doctrine off the page and giving it life. Without institutional support, tort law would be much more inert than it is. On the other hand, it is probably safe to say that law's institutional resources are more important for detecting, investigating and remedying breaches of tort law ('torts') than for securing conformity to the law. As we will see in Chapter 9, it is commonly argued that tort law is useful partly to encourage people to act in certain desirable ways and deter them from acting in other undesirable (tortious) ways. However, there is an important difference between conformity and compliance: a person's behaviour may conform to law regardless of whether that person is motivated to comply with the law (Stone 2016). Conformity is merely acting as the law requires for whatever reason. Compliance is doing what the law requires *because* the law requires it. If we take seriously the probability that most people know very little tort doctrine and understand very little about how legal institutions work, conduct in conformity with the law is more likely to be the result of compliance with extra-legal norms— notably norms of personal (and social) morality—than with legal norms. Whatever the strengths of legal institutions, they may have relatively little to contribute to securing compliance with law. At the same time, however, in some matters the law plays such a large role in supplementing broad, moral norms that people frequently seek advice in advance about how to conform to the law. Good examples are taxation, and buying and selling land and buildings. In such contexts, perhaps, conformity is typically underpinned by a motivation to comply. Again, we may suppose, when people drive on the correct side of the road and obey speed limits they are typically complying with the law, not merely conforming to it.

3

Torts

KI 2: Tort law is the law of torts

Just as the proposition discussed in the previous chapter—that 'tort law is law'—contains an important truth, so does the—superficially banal—idea that tort law is the law of torts. Look at the contents pages of a standard tort law textbook. There you will find more-or-less puzzling headings such as Trespass, Nuisance, Conversion, Defamation, Conspiracy, Negligence, Occupiers' Liability, Product Liability and so on. Each of these names 'a tort'. Together, the recognised torts (more than 30 on one recent count: Mulheron 2016, 2–7) are a bit of a rag-bag. The first five items on the list just given apparently refer to specific types of conduct. 'Negligence' looks more like a way of way of acting—negligently as opposed to carefully—rather than any specific action. The last two items apparently relate to activities—occupation (of land) and being involved (in some unspecified way) with products.

Next, for a contrast, look at the contents pages of a standard contract law textbook. Everything, here, seems much more logical and coherent. The various chapters are all concerned, in one way or another, with this one thing called a 'contract'—making contracts, interpreting contracts, breach of contract, remedying breaches of contracts, and so on. Some contract books will also tell you about specific types of contract, such as contracts of sale, contracts of hire, employment contracts, and so on. But these are different *types* of the one thing called 'a contract'—they are not different 'contracts'. Lawyers normally think of contract law as the law of contract (singular), not the law of contracts (plural).

Now, third, look at the contents pages of a standard criminal law textbook. The chapters typically fall into two broad categories. The first group of chapters, which may be called 'general principles' or 'the general part', deal with matters such as the elements of a crime (*mens rea* and *actus reus*), defences, parties to crime (corporations, accomplices and the rest), sentencing, and so on. The second group of chapters, which may be headed 'specific offences' or 'the special part', name offences—murder, theft and so on—and discuss them as applications of the general principles surveyed in the first part.

Finally, go back to the tort law textbook. Here you will find no 'general part' and, typically, only a brief and rather desultory attempt, in the first chapter, to 'define' the word 'tort', together with a discussion of things that torts are *not*, notably crimes and breaches of contract. This might give the impression that tort law is a residual category, a sort of random collection of things that don't belong anywhere else, but without anything much to bind them together except the covers of the book. How did this rather odd situation come about?

Tort law is one of the many 'areas of law' into which lawyers divide the large body of English law to make it easier to understand, teach and use. Other areas of law, besides criminal law and contract law, include constitutional law and property law. Most people have a serviceable, if rough, understanding of what we mean by a 'crime', a 'constitution', a 'contract', and 'property'. These are all words used more-or-less frequently in everyday speech with meanings related to their more precise legal counterparts. By contrast, only lawyers use the word 'tort' with any regularity or familiarity. And yet tort law is relevant to a wide range of common phenomena as diverse as industrial disputes, scurrilous newspaper articles, transport accidents, noisy neighbours, dangerous pharmaceutical drugs, vicious dogs, and so on. The word 'tort' is derived, through French, from a Latin word commonly translated as 'wrong'. However, this is not a very useful translation because on the one hand, not all conduct that the law considers wrongful is 'tortious' (in other words, not all legal wrongs are 'torts': **KI 4**). For instance, crimes and breaches of contract can also be called legal 'wrongs'. On the other hand, not all torts consist of conduct that would commonly be called or considered 'wrongful'. For instance, trespassing on another's land is a legal wrong—a tort—even if the 'trespasser' reasonably and honestly believed that the land was their own and that they were entitled to be there.

Although some of the situations tort law deals with are features particularly of the modern world, many have been characteristic of social life since the birth of the English legal system, which we can date, notionally, at 1066. However, the concept of 'tort law' as a legal category was invented only in the latter half of the nineteenth century when scholars began organising law into 'areas'. Before that, English law was divided up differently and organised along 'formulary' lines. At the heart of the 'formulary system' were 'writs'. These were the documents by which court actions were begun, equivalent to what we would now call a 'statement of claim'. A writ has been helpfully compared to 'a modern administrative form, with preprinted sets of words corresponding to the claim they are used to make, and dotted lines the applicant will fill in to explain the particulars of his case' (Descheemaeker 2009, 191). Lawyers thought of 'the particulars' of the claim (that is, what it was about) in terms of 'causes of action'—nuisance, libel, trespass and so on. The writ was the 'form of action', and each cause of action had a corresponding form, which had to be used to make a claim based on that cause. Use the wrong form and no matter how good the claim in substance, it would fail because of the defective form (think of visa applications today!); and if there was no appropriate form of action, there was no cause of action.

The formulary system was abolished in England in the nineteenth century. This development shifted attention away from form and onto substance. It encouraged new thinking about the principles underlying the various causes of action that were no longer encased in the forms of action. The process is well illustrated by the development of tort liability for negligence. The concept of 'negligent conduct' as a basis of tort liability began to emerge early in the nineteenth century, before the abolition of the formulary system, as a response to new social problems of industrialisation, such as increasing numbers of road accidents. Later in the century, some jurists (a useful word to use to refer collectively to judges and legal scholars) argued for recognition of a general principle of liability for negligent conduct. By contrast, others thought that liability for negligence should be framed in terms of various discrete relationships such as doctor and patient, occupier of land and visitor, carrier and passenger; and by reference to the various different activities associated with such relationships (such as providing medical care or occupying land). This latter, category-based (or 'functional') approach had more in common with older, formulary, ways of thinking than did the 'principle-based' (or 'conceptual') approach.

In fact, both approaches are still reflected in modern tort law. What we call 'torts'—defamation, deceit, trespass, nuisance, and so on—are the modern counterparts of the old causes of action. What's more, the category-based approach that refers to relationships and activities is still reflected in discrete elements of tort law referred to as 'occupiers' liability', 'employers' liability' and 'product liability', for instance. It is this that leads to the idea that we have a law of *torts* (plural), not a law of *tort* (singular). At the same time, it is reasonably accurate to say that the modern law embodies a general principle of liability for negligent conduct. Ironically, however, the prime manifestation of the negligence principle is the so-called 'tort' of negligence. The development of this modern 'cause of action' *post*-dated the abolition of the formulary system and culminated only in 1932 in the decision of the House of Lords in *Donoghue* v *Stevenson* [1932] AC 562. What's more, modern tort law contains no general principle of liability for causing harm intentionally, and no general principle governing when conduct can amount to a tort regardless of whether it was intentional or negligent—or, as it is more usually put, when 'strict liability' can arise. Instead, the issue of the 'standard of liability' is resolved piecemeal in relation to each particular tort (except the tort of negligence, under which only negligent conduct can be tortious). The peculiarity of the tort of negligence is that it is the only tort based on a standard of liability as such. At the same time, negligence is sometimes the standard of liability in other torts, such as trespass; and in relation to some torts, the standard of liability may vary according to the factual circumstances of the case being considered. For instance, the standard of liability for trespass to land may vary according to whether or not the landowner claims that the trespasser not only entered the land without permission but also damaged the land or things on the land.

The upshot of all this is that there is no obvious or easy answer to the questions, 'what is a tort?' and 'what (if anything) do all torts have in common?' Although the law has a reasonably coherent legal concept of 'a contract', we have no similarly coherent legal concept of 'a tort'. We know that torts can die and that new torts can be born. For instance, the old tort of 'detinue', which existed for centuries, was killed off by statute in 1977. In recent years, a new tort of 'harassment' appears to have been created. But because we lack understanding of the basic nature of the wrongs that the law calls 'torts', there can be arguments about whether or not a particular tort exists. For instance, no one really knows whether 'breach of confidence' and 'invasion of privacy' are, or are not, torts. This can cause problems because, as we have noted, torts are only one species of legal wrong, and it sometimes matters in practice whether a particular wrong belongs to the species 'tort' or to some other species, such as 'breach of contract' (for more on this see Barker, Cane, Lunney and Trindade 2012, 6–10). Perhaps the best we can say is that a tort is what legal institutions with the power to make tort law (Parliament and courts) say is 'a tort'. After all, the word 'tort' is legal jargon, not a term in use outside the law.

It has to be admitted, however, that this conclusion is rather unsatisfying. Saying 'torts are what lawyers call torts' leads inexorably to that most typical of children's questions: why? It is not surprising, therefore, that some scholars have tried to identify a characteristic that all the recognised torts share. For instance, it has been argued that what makes all tortious conduct 'wrong' is that it involves one person putting themselves 'in charge of another' (Ripstein 2016). Some scholars have said that the common characteristic shared by all torts is that they protect 'rights' (for example, Stevens 2007); while others describe the golden thread that runs through tort law as a purpose or use such as 'compensating for harm', or 'deterring wrongful conduct', or doing 'corrective justice' between the parties. The last of these mooted uses has been particularly popular in recent years (for example, Weinrib 1995), while the second-last (that tort law provides incentives to behave in certain ways and not in others) attracted a lot of followers in the 1960s and 1970s (for example, Posner (first published) 1973) but never really took off outside the USA. Here is not the place to explore such approaches in any great detail. They are all subject to much debate and disagreement. One problem they pose is that the various suggested unifying explanatory features of tort law are so abstract that they can be used equally well to explain contract law, for example, or the whole of 'private law' (of which tort law is a part: see more on this in Chapter 6). Another problem is that despite the elasticity of the suggested common features, their proponents sometimes end up concluding that the chosen feature cannot explain all torts and all aspects of tort law. A solution offered for this problem is an argument along the lines that the torts or aspects of tort law that the chosen feature cannot explain are wrongly classified by lawyers as torts, or parts of tort law, and that they properly belong to some other legal category. Unfortunately, such arguments tell us what their authors think tort law *should be* rather than what lawyers say it *is*.

It is unlikely that a satisfactory 'grand unifying theory' of the nature of a tort and tort law will ever be found; and the reasons are easy to find. Law is what we might call a 'cumulative' phenomenon. This means that once a legal rule or principle is made by an official or an institution with the power to make tort law, it will remain part of the law until it is 'unmade'. So, for instance, Acts of Parliament remain 'on the statute book' until 'repealed' by Parliament. The English statute book contains some very old statutes that are still in force, such as the Bill of Rights Act 1689. The basic provisions of the Fatal Accidents Act 1976 (an extremely important statute dealing with aspects of tort law) were first enacted in 1846 and have remained in force since then because they have never been repealed; and the 1976 version of the statute has been amended various times since it was first enacted in that form. Some judicial decisions have similar staying power. The foundational decision in 'modern' tort law—*Donoghue v Stevenson*—is now almost a century old, and there are many cases decided in the eighteenth and nineteenth centuries that still form an important part of current tort law.

The tort law of today is a complex amalgam of law-making over a period of centuries by many different judges and many successive Parliaments, as interpreted by scholars and applied by courts. The cumulative nature of (tort) law enables it to perform an important function, of securing settled continuity of social normative practices, which is critical to stable and successful human life. On the other hand, the ability of law-makers to change the law allows law to perform the equally important function of keeping social normative practices abreast of changing circumstances and changing values. For instance, the dramatic social changes associated with industrialisation in the nineteenth century were reflected in equally radical changes in the law, including tort law. In more recent decades, changes of ideology associated with the transition, in the 1980s and 1990s, from the politics of the welfare state in its heyday after World War II, to the more individualistic values of 'neo-liberalism', have (arguably, anyway) also brought about changes in tort law. Our current tort law is the evolved product of the activities of many law-makers over a very long period. We would not expect such a process to generate a highly coherent and unified body of law. We could liken tort law to a patchwork quilt, gradually sown together by a group of quilters, then used and repaired for generations: all the patches will have some things in common (although perhaps not very many), but the differences between them are just as important as any similarities to our appreciation of the whole quilt.

Remember, too, that tort law is partly the work of legal scholars who write the tort books. The shape of tort law owes a lot to the writers of the first tort texts in the late nineteenth century. Although Parliament and courts make discrete rules and principles of tort law, that law as a whole has never been consolidated or stated in one place by any law-making institution. Therefore, when we try to understand 'tort law', our subject is, in an important sense, an invention of scholars with no official law-making role. Scholars who attempt to find unifying theories of tort law are engaged in a similar task to that undertaken by the early textbook writers: trying to decide what *ought to be* included in a tort book and what ought to be left out. There is no official, 'legal' answer to this question because law-makers do not write law books. Put differently, perhaps, there is no 'formal code of tort law' which sets out all the basic rules and principles of tort law in one place.

For such reasons, the strategy adopted in this book (and worked out in the next two chapters) for deepening the reader's understanding of tort law is not to look for a unitary theory to explain all its components and features but rather to provide a sort of 'structural' account that acknowledges the historical process of legal development and preserves its internal diversity but also brings out some recurring patterns. The aim is to allow the reader to rise above the fine-grained detail of the law and to discern a larger picture, but without making any claim that this perspective reveals that the contents of tort books have a deep organic unity or that there is a legal equivalent of the physicists' holy grail—the 'elementary particle' from which everything is built.

4

Torts Unpacked

KI 3: Each tort has two main elements:

(1) conduct that is classified by tort law as wrongful and

(2) one or more interests with which that conduct has interfered in ways specified by tort law

The strategy in this chapter is to unpack the inherited causes of action ('torts') into two components. In the next chapter, these components will be put back together again in a different pattern. This should make the internal operation and structure of tort law clearer than does its traditional division into causes of action called 'torts'. The aim is to breathe some life into the tort doctrine on the pages of the tort books by uncovering what it can tell us about human social life.

Tort law starts with the idea that human beings have interests that are vulnerable to being 'interfered with' or 'harmed by' human conduct. Harmful conduct might be that of the very person whose interest is harmed, or it might be conduct of another person. Tort law, we might say, is about certain types of harmful interferences with certain types of interests. A tort is a harmful interference by one person—let's call that person the 'harm-doer'—with an interest of another person—let's call that person the 'harm-sufferer'. As already noted, not all harmful interferences with legally protected interests of another are tortious. Furthermore, while a person may harm an interest of their own, self-harm is not tortious. However, conduct of the harm-sufferer can affect the legal position of a harm-doer by wholly or partly relieving the harm-doer of legal liability. Tort law, like contract law, is about—and only about—how individual people interact with other individuals. This is not true of criminal law, for instance. Some crimes—such as drug possession—are 'victimless' in the sense that the law prohibits certain conduct regardless of whether it interferes with or harms the interests of any other person. By contrast, there are no 'victimless torts'.

We are all, at one and the same time, both potential harm-doers and potential harm-sufferers. Tort law is concerned, positively, with the interests we all share as potential harm-sufferers but also, negatively, with the interest in freedom of action we all share, as potential harm-doers. 'Autonomy'—being free to live one's life as one wants—is perhaps the fundamental political and legal value of modern Western culture. By branding certain conduct as tortious, the law interferes with that interest. We accept this on condition that the law should interfere with our interest in freedom of action only to the extent necessary and reasonable for successful social life. Tort law, we may say, is concerned to protect our interests as potential harm-sufferers, but only to the extent consistent with leaving us, as potential harm-doers, with a reasonable amount of freedom of action. In tort law, freedom from harm and freedom of action are, as it were, in equilibrium: the interest in freedom from harm marks the boundaries of the interest in freedom of action (and vice-versa).

We will begin the chapter by looking at the interests, protected by tort law, that we all share as potential harm-sufferers. In the second part, we will examine the interest in reasonable freedom of action that tort law accords to us all as potential harm-doers. We will, in addition, mention some other interests of potential harm-doers and of society to which tort law offers some protection.

1. PROTECTED INTERESTS OF POTENTIAL HARM-SUFFERERS

INTERESTS IN BODY AND MIND

Tort law recognises that every human being has an interest in good health and in being whole in body and mind. However, it also insists that any life is better than none, and so does not allow 'wrongful life' claims in which a child seeks to recover from a doctor damages for having been born disabled as a result of negligent failure by the doctor to alert the mother to the risk of the child being born disabled, thus depriving her of the chance to seek a therapeutic abortion. Furthermore, of course, tort law does not allow actions by healthy children complaining of having been born as a result of a failed abortion or sterilisation. (Somewhat inconsistently, however, the law protects parents in both types of case from having to bear the financial and emotional cost of rearing a disabled or unwanted child.)

In theory, tort law does not distinguish between disease (such as cancer) and ill-health (such as bronchitis) on the one hand, and traumatic injuries (such as cuts and bruises or the loss of a limb) on the other. In practice, however, the interest in freedom from traumatic injury is much better protected than interests in freedom from disease and illness (Stapleton 1986). An important reason for this is that it is often harder to establish the precise cause of an illness or disease than a trauma and, so, harder to prove that it resulted from tortious behaviour by an identifiable individual.

On the other hand, tort law does distinguish formally between injury to the body (including the brain) and injury to the mind. It gives more protection to the body than to the mind by being more ready to recognise bodily injury as harm than to classify mental injury in this way. This distinction between physical injuries and mental injuries probably reflects more general social attitudes towards mental illness, which many people are more inclined to think of as just the way 'normal' people sometimes are, rather than as the result of anything that might have been done or happened to them. Another reason why the law distinguishes between body and mind may be that in general, it is less easy for the external observer to verify a person's mental state than their physical condition, because we know relatively little about the relationship between the brain and mental states. Finally, the distinction probably reflects a common feeling that people can reasonably be expected to put up with mental problems more than with physical problems.

Tort law distinguishes two types of mental injury. One is actionable only if the victim has suffered some other type of actionable injury as well; and the other may be actionable even if that is the only injury that a person has suffered. Mental suffering of the first type is commonly called 'pain and suffering' in cases where it accompanies physical injury; and 'anxiety and inconvenience' when it accompanies damage to property or financial loss (for example, *Attia v British Gas* [1988] QB 304). Mental suffering of the second type is commonly called 'nervous shock'. A more accurate alternative phrase is 'medically recognised psychiatric illness'.

This phrase pinpoints the crucial difference between the two types of mental suffering: the second type is suffering recognised by the medical profession as ill-health or injury, whereas the first type need not be beyond the limits of what are accepted as normal mental reactions to external events or stimuli. The term 'nervous shock' is first found in early-twentieth-century cases in which liability for mental suffering was first allowed. These were cases in which people suffered a 'shock' as a result of being involved in or witnessing horrific accidents. Now mental injury may, in certain cases, form the basis of a tort action even if it is not the result of a shock in this sense.

Tort law, then, takes two quite different approaches to mental injury. It will react to mental injury standing alone only if it is medically recognised as abnormal; whereas, if mental injury is accompanied by some other actionable injury, tort law will react to it even though the injured person's mental state would not be described as abnormal.

Nervous shock is itself divided into two types depending on whether or not it is a 'direct' result of a tort. An example of 'direct nervous shock' would be 'stress-induced' mental illness resulting from an excessive workload imposed on an employee by an employer (for example, *Barber v Somerset CC* [2004] 1 WLR 1089). Another example would be mental illness suffered by the occupant of a car as a result of being involved in a road accident; or by a rescuer as a result of helping at the scene of an accident. If the harm-doer's conduct created a foreseeable risk that the harm-sufferer would be caused bodily (as opposed to mental) injury, the harm-doer can be held liable for direct nervous shock suffered by the harm-sufferer even if it was so abnormal a reaction to the tort that it could be described as 'unforeseeable', and even if, in fact, the harm-sufferer suffered no bodily injury (*Page v Smith* [1996] AC 155). Victims of direct nervous shock are called 'primary victims'. Indirect nervous shock is shock suffered as a result of witnessing (even passively) the plight of primary victims of physical or mental injury (*Alcock v Chief Constable of South Yorkshire* [1992] 1 AC 310). Victims of indirect nervous shock are called 'secondary victims'.

Tort law gives much less protection to secondary victims of mental injury than to primary victims. First, the secondary victim's mental suffering must have been the result of suffering a 'shock' in a colloquial sense. This means, for instance, that a secondary victim is not protected against psychiatric illness resulting from caring for an injured person over a long period of time. Second, the secondary victim's mental injury must not have been so abnormal that it was not 'reasonably foreseeable'. Third, the secondary victim must (as a general rule) have been in a relationship of 'love and affection' with the primary victim. Some relationships (such as parent and child) are assumed to be relationships of love and affection, but others (such as aunt and nephew) will only qualify as such if the secondary victim can prove that they enjoyed close ties of love and affection with the primary victim. Fourth, the secondary victim must have witnessed the shocking incident or its 'aftermath' personally; shock suffered as a result of receiving merely verbal reports is not actionable, although watching live TV coverage of an incident might count as personal observation. There is no precise definition of 'aftermath', but it is said to refer to phenomena that were quite close in time and space to the incident.

The rationale for these limitations on liability to secondary victims is unclear, and many people find them unsatisfactory and even repugnant. How can we justify a rule that requires mentally traumatised people to go to court and prove that they have strong feelings of love and affection towards another? But how ought the law to be changed? One approach might be to abolish liability to secondary victims or even to all victims of nervous shock standing alone (Stapleton 1994b, 95–96). Diametrically opposed is an approach which would allow any victim of reasonably foreseeable nervous shock to recover (Mullany and Handford 1993). Various intermediate positions involving reform of some of the rules about secondary victims but not others could be imagined and might appeal to some people.

DIGNITARY INTERESTS

Tort law protects people not only from bodily and mental injury but also from attacks on their 'dignity' and on those aspects of their life and personality that define their individuality. For example, depriving a person of liberty may be tortious. Unwanted physical contact may be tortious even though it causes no bodily injury if, for instance, it is of an intimate nature. Invading a person's privacy by entering their land without their consent may be tortious.

For much of its history, tort law was mainly concerned with protecting people from physical injury and from interference with their tangible property. The only dignitary interests to which tort law offered significant protection were personal liberty and reputation. Social demands for legal protection against invasions of privacy and sexual harassment, for instance, are quite recent. In the absence of action by Parliament, the courts have found it difficult (because of the legacy of formularism) to develop tort law to provide such protection. A good illustration of this difficulty is provided by the courts' response to the problem of stalking. Stalking may not cause bodily injury or a recognised psychiatric illness and it may involve no intrusion onto the victim's land. In several cases, courts toyed with the idea of creating a new tort of 'harassment', but eventually Parliament stepped in with the Protection from Harassment Act 1997. A particularly striking example of the shortcomings of the formulary approach is provided by *Kaye v Robertson* [1991] FSR 62 in which a celebrity was badly injured in an accident. Journalists, ignoring a 'restricted visiting' sign on the door of his hospital room, photographed him in bed and 'interviewed' him. A rather lurid story was subsequently published about him in their newspaper. The court thought that the journalists were guilty of a gross invasion of privacy, but the only basis in tort law which could be found for a decision in the celebrity's favour was the obscure tort of 'injurious falsehood'. On this basis, the harm-doers' wrong was not invading the harm-sufferer's privacy but, rather, implying in their article his consent to its publication had been obtained. This, it was said, damaged his professional reputation by suggesting that he would do 'anything for money'. To this day, there is no 'tort of invasion of privacy' as such, although the law does protect against certain invasions of privacy such as unjustified disclosure of private information.

By contrast, tort law has protected reputation for centuries. This it does chiefly through liability for defamation. A person's reputation is what other people think of the person as opposed to the person's pride or sense of self-worth. A defamatory statement is one that would tend to lead 'right-thinking people' to think less of its subject or lead them to 'shun or avoid' that person. Notice the use of the words 'would tend' in this definition: one of the most curious aspects of the law of defamation is that it imposes liability not for damaging a person's reputation but for making a statement that the court thinks could damage the person's reputation. The claimant in a defamation action need present no evidence of actual damage to reputation. One result of this rule is that defamation claimants are often viewed as 'gold-diggers', more interested in their hurt feelings and their bank-balances than with any negative impact on their reputations. Indeed, the accusation is sometimes made that a defamation action is being used as a source of publicity and to enhance the claimant's future prospects rather than to recover lost esteem. In other words, although defamation is formally concerned with reputation, the rule that proof of damage to reputation is not necessary means that in practice, defamation claims are often more concerned with things other than reputation.

CIVIL AND POLITICAL INTERESTS

One of the major legal developments of the twentieth century has been the widespread adoption of 'bills of rights' embodying, above all, civil and political rights such as freedom of speech, freedom of movement and association, and personal liberty, which are fundamental to active citizenship. Of the main civil liberties protected by modern bills of rights, the common law of tort has traditionally protected the right to vote (*Ashby v White* (1794) 6 Mod 45) and personal liberty. Wrongful arrest and wrongful imprisonment are torts which, for centuries, have been used to counter abuse of public (and private) power. Interference with freedom of speech or with freedom of movement and association have never, as such, been heads of tort liability. However, as we will see later in the chapter, these interests (in the guise of 'the public interest') are sometimes protected in ways that benefit potential harm-doers.

PROPERTY INTERESTS

Common-Law and Equitable Property

One of the most important uses of tort law is to protect interests in tangible and intangible property. Property law creates property interests and tort law protects them. Not all the sorts of interests people can have in relation to property are property interests. Most importantly, a person can have a contractual right to use property without having a property interest 'in' that property. Contractual interests are considered later. Tangible property is either 'real' or 'personal'. Real property is land and things attached to it. Personal property (also called 'chattels') is moveable. Intangible property is anything that lacks a physical form and over which the law grants people property rights. Examples include patents, trademarks and other 'intellectual property rights', and debts.

To understand the role of tort law in protecting property rights, it is necessary to distinguish between 'common law' and the law of 'equity'. For many centuries (until the nineteenth century) there were two distinct sets of courts in England—common-law courts and equity courts. The equity courts developed out of a medieval practice of litigants, who were dissatisfied with a decision of one of the King's ('common-law') courts, of petitioning the Lord Chancellor (effectively, the King's prime minister) to force the successful party to act 'equitably' in relation to the petitioner. Gradually, this practice was formalised and the Court of Chancery was established. The rules of 'equity' made and administered by the Chancery Court were effectively glosses on the body of common law administered by the King's courts, designed to make good inadequacies or injustices in the common law. Perhaps the most important invention of the Chancery court was the 'trust'. Put simply, the trust is a device that allows an owner (the 'settlor') to transfer ownership of property (the 'trust property') to another (the 'trustee') on condition that the trustee manage it for the benefit of ('in trust for') a third party (the 'beneficiary'). Whereas the common-law courts would allow the trustee to treat the property as their own, Chancery was prepared to enforce the condition in favour of the beneficiary. The trustee was said to be the 'legal owner' of the trust property and the beneficiary was the 'equitable owner'. In other words, the trustee had a 'legal' property interest in the trust property while the beneficiary had an 'equitable' property interest. Both tangible and intangible property could be put 'into trust', but the 'equitable property' belonging to the beneficiary was always intangible—it was, in effect, a right to enforce the terms of the trust against the trustee 'in Chancery'. The result of this institutional history is that property 'torts' protect only against interference with legal property; wrongful interference with equitable property is not a tort but an 'equitable wrong'.

Tort law was developed by the common-law courts. In the formative years of the common law, only tangible things were recognised as 'property'. Most torts that protect interests in intangible property—notably 'intellectual property' such as patents, trademarks, copyright and design rights—were created much later by statute. The prime use of intellectual property rights is to facilitate control by the owner of the commercial exploitation of fruits of intellectual effort. Infringements of intellectual property rights are not normally discussed in the context of tort law but they are, in effect, 'statutory torts'.

The statutory tort of infringement of a trademark effectively protects what is called 'goodwill' by protecting marks that attract business to their owners. Goodwill itself (the power to attract customers) is also protected by the common-law tort called 'passing-off'. Passing-off involves one person misrepresenting that another person's goods or services are their own. The common-law tort of passing-off protects goodwill as such by treating it as a form of property. The statutory tort of infringement of a trade mark protects goodwill indirectly by treating business-attracting marks (rather than the goodwill itself) as property. The common-law courts never developed torts that could be used to protect copyright and patents.

What is 'Interference with Property'?

The legal concept of 'property' is a very tricky one. In one sense, property is things. But not all things are property in the legal sense. For instance, the air we breathe is not anyone's property, and in a society where slavery is prohibited, living human beings are not property. To say that something is property in the legal sense is to say that people can have certain rights and obligations 'over' it that are recognised as 'incidents of property'. Tort law protects property from various forms of interference, each of which relates to one of the incidents of property.

The basic interest in property protected by tort law is 'possession', not 'ownership' (or 'title'). To be 'in possession' is to have control of the property or the right to control it. For example, for the duration of a lease of real property, the lessor does not have a right to control the property and so can be liable in tort for dispossessing the tenant. Depriving a person of (the right to) possession is called 'misappropriation', and only property that can be possessed—tangible property—can be misappropriated. Misappropriation involves taking another's (moveable) property away from them, or taking possession of another's (immoveable) property. But conduct will amount to misappropriation only if it is inconsistent with that other person's interest in the property. For example, one person may use another's pen without misappropriating it. 'Trespass to land' is the tort of misappropriating real property. A colloquial term for misappropriation of real property is 'squatting'. 'Conversion' is the tort of misappropriating chattels.

A second 'incident of property' is the right to exploit it. Unauthorised exploitation of property falling short of misappropriation may be a tort.

To exploit property is to make use of it for one's benefit. Examples of exploitation of real property include using land for access, or for parking, or for tipping waste; invasions of airspace by signs (for example, *Kelsen v Imperial Tobacco Co (of Great Britain and Northern Ireland) Ltd* [1957] 2 QB 334) or the jibs of cranes (for example, *Woollerton v Richard Costain Ltd* [1970] 1 WLR 411); and the placing of scaffolding on adjoining land to facilitate building work (for example, *John Trenberth v National West- minster Bank Ltd* (1980) 39 P & CR 104). 'Joyriding' would be an example of exploitation of a chattel. Exploitation of land or goods may amount to the tort of trespass. Passing-off also involves exploitation of property, in this case the goodwill of a business.

A third incident of property is the right to 'use and enjoy' it. No tort directly protects the right to use and enjoy chattels; but depriving some- one of the use of a chattel, for instance, might be actionable as a trespass or conversion. The most important tort that protects the use and enjoy- ment of real property from interference is private nuisance, which is an *unreasonable* interference with the use and enjoyment of land. Typical examples are noisy neighbours and factory emissions. Such interference may result in damage to the land itself, financial loss (as in the case of a hotel blighted by noise), or 'amenity damage'. 'Amenity' refers to the pleasure and enjoyment which people get out of their property. Some aspects of the enjoyment of land are not protected. For instance, blocking a view cannot be a nuisance; nor can interference with TV transmission by the construction of a building (*Hunter v Canary Wharf Ltd* [1997] AC 655). Private nuisance only protects the use and enjoyment of people with property interests in the land; effectively, this means owners and tenants. For instance, it is not a tort to interfere with the use and enjoy- ment of mere occupants, such as members of an owner's or lessee's family, even if their use and enjoyment of the property is just as affected as that of the owner or lessee. This rule is a function of the theory that nuisance is interference with property rights rather than interference with use and enjoyment as such.

A fourth incident of property is the right to freedom from damage. In the case of tangible property, the damage in question is physical; and it includes destruction or loss. It is also possible to 'damage' intangible property in the sense of reducing its value. For instance, one actiona- ble form of infringement of a trademark is called 'dilution'. The power of a trademark is to attract people to buy the goods or services of the mark-owner. If an identifying mark is used widely enough, it may lose its drawing power. This has happened in the case of the word 'hoover', which in popular usage has become a synonym for 'vacuum cleaner' rather than the identifying name of a vacuum cleaner made by one particular manufacturer. Whereas exploitation of a trademark involves taking advantage of the drawing power of the mark, damaging it by dilution consists of reducing its drawing power. A common-law tort concerned with damage to intangible property is injurious (or 'malicious') falsehood. Injurious falsehood is, in effect, commercial defamation. The property in question is goodwill, and the damage is reducing the power to attract customers by making a false statement about a person's goods, services, business or occupation.

CONTRACTUAL INTERESTS

Contractual rights are rights under existing contracts (as opposed to the chance of making a contract in the future). A contract is a legally enforceable arrangement for transferring resources (property or services) from one person to another. Most of the legal rules which can be used to protect contractual rights are treated as part of the law of contract. However, there are some rules of tort law that provide such protection. Tort law may protect a contracting party against conduct detrimental to the party's rights under the contract done by the other contracting party ('breach of contract'), or done by a 'third party', that is, someone not a party to the contract.

In general, tort law does not protect contractual rights over property (such as the right to use property) but only 'proprietary' rights, such as possession. Protecting contractual rights over property is the province of contract law. However, tort law does protect against third-party infringement of rights under contracts not concerned with the use of property (such as contracts for the sale of goods or the provision of services). The tort of 'interference with contract' protects against action by one person (D) that results in non-performance by A of a contract between C and A, causing financial loss to C. D's action might consist of inducing A not to comply with the contract by persuasion or threats ('intimidation'), or D might disable A from complying with the contract.

In addition to such protection against third-party interference, conduct that amounts to a breach of contract (by the other party to the contract) may amount to a tort. In particular, negligent breaches of contract may also be actionable as tortious negligence. Tort law does not protect against any and every breach of contract. For instance, many breaches of contract consist not of harmful actions ('misfeasance', or 'causing harm') but of harmful failures to act ('omissions', or 'nonfeasance', or 'failing to prevent harm'). In general, tort law provides less protection against non-feasance than against misfeasance. The typical breach of contract which is also a tort is negligent misfeasance in the performance of services. In such cases, tort law protects the same interest as contract law, namely the interest in careful performance of the contract.

Tort law provides some protection for 'contractual expectancies'—that is, opportunities to make advantageous contracts in the future and to make financial or other gains by contracting. Tort liability for misstatements which induce a person to enter a contract protects a person's interest in not making a contract in the mistaken belief that it will be more advantageous than it in fact turns out to be. Tort liability for contract-inducing misstatements may attach to the other party to the contract or to a third party.

Torts such as 'intimidation' and '(unlawful means) conspiracy' provide protection against 'unlawful' conduct done with the intention of interfering with a person's opportunities for contracting. The purpose of such interference will typically be to prevent one person contracting with another or to 'force' the harm-sufferer to contract with the interferer, or both. Such conduct is often called 'interference with business' or 'interference with trade'. A rather different form of liability for interference with the opportunity to contract can arise under statutes such as the Sex Discrimination Act 1975 and the Race Relations Act 1976, one of the aims of which is to create statutory tort-like causes of action for refusal to contract with a person because, respectively, of their sex or race.

NON-CONTRACTUAL EXPECTANCIES

Tort law may protect opportunities of receiving financial gain in the future by means other than entering an advantageous contract. For example, if a provision in a will giving a legacy to an intended beneficiary is legally invalid because of some defect in the will resulting from the negligence of a legal adviser, the beneficiary may recover the value of the intended legacy from the lawyer (*White v Jones* [1995] 2 AC 207). More important, perhaps, is the protection given to family members deprived of continuing financial support by the death of another member of the family. Under the Fatal Accidents Act 1976 'dependants' of a person who has been wrongfully killed have a cause of action in tort to recover for loss of (actual and) expected financial support from that person.

WEALTH

Property rights and contractual rights are wealth-producing assets; and in a market economy, the opportunity (freedom) to make contracts is the chief legal technique for wealth-creation. One way in which tort law protects wealth is by protecting wealth-creating assets; and one of the ways it does *this* is by compensating for financial loss (that is, reductions of wealth) caused by certain sorts of interferences with wealth-creating assets. Tort law also provides some protection to wealth in its own right— the 'capital' which a person's wealth-generating assets represent and produce. In other words, sometimes tort law makes good reductions of wealth without reference to any asset which represents or generated that wealth. For instance, in the tort of deceit, a fraudster may be held liable for having induced another to give money away; and in certain circumstances, tort law provides protection against paying more than its value for a substandard service or item of property. This residual category of cases in which tort law protects the interest in wealth as such is very small. Most heads of tort liability protect one or other of the interests discussed above.

2. 'COUNTERVAILING' PUBLIC AND PRIVATE INTERESTS

Beside the interest in freedom of action that we all share (considered later), tort law also protects, and juxtaposes to the interests of potential harm-sufferers, certain other interests that we share as potential harm-doers ('private interests') and as members of society ('public interests').

The protection given to some countervailing public interests takes the form of providing harm-doers with defences to tort claims. Statutory provisions that 'authorise' conduct which might otherwise be tortious are an important source of such defences. Common-law public interest defences to defamation claims (truth, absolute and qualified privilege, and fair comment) play an important part in protecting freedom of speech and information. There are also defences to claims for wrongful arrest and imprisonment to promote maintenance of law and order.

Other countervailing public interests are protected not by defences but by immunities. Whereas defences typically focus on the harm-doer's conduct, immunities typically reflect the harm-doer's status. And whereas a defence only becomes relevant after the harm-doer's conduct has been adjudged tortious, an immunity prevents a person's conduct being subjected to scrutiny in a tort action. For instance, participants in court proceedings (judges, advocates, witnesses, litigants) enjoy an immunity from tort liability in respect of things said and done by them in those proceedings. MPs enjoy absolute privilege in the law of defamation in respect of things said in 'proceedings in Parliament'. Public bodies (such as regulatory agencies) may enjoy statutory immunity from tort liability for negligence, and there is a complex body of judge-made law designed to immunise 'policy' decisions of public bodies from tort liability.

The protection of public interests by tort law reflects the fact that human beings are social animals. Although some of our interactions with other people have few if any social ramifications (and in that sense are purely private), many of our dealings with others can only be properly understood in their social context. More particularly, the significance of harm-causing conduct can be affected by its social value. For instance, the significance of publication by a newspaper of a true but damaging story about a prominent political figure is assessed in light of society's legitimate interest in knowing the truth about its politicians. In publishing the truth, the newspaper is acting, as it were, on behalf of society and not just in its own commercial interests. The social interest in the conduct strengthens the personal interest that the publisher has in freedom of action.

Defences designed to protect private interests of potential harm-doers include self-defence (an answer to liability for intentional infliction of personal injury), defence of property (a defence to liability for deliberate entry onto land and intentional infliction of personal injury), necessity (an answer to a claim for intentional or negligent damage to property), and justification (an answer to liability for intentional infliction of economic harm where the harm-doer's motive was to protect his or her own legitimate financial interests).

There is another very important personal countervailing interest recognised by tort law, namely freedom of contract. The basic rule is that a person is free to contract with another to limit or exclude the person's potential liability in tort to the other. This freedom has been considerably modified by statute. For example, under the Unfair Contract Terms Act 1977, a term in a contract designed to exclude or restrict liability for negligently-caused personal injury is ineffective; and a clause purporting to exclude liability for any other type of damage negligently caused is only effective to the extent that the clause is 'reasonable'. The main thrust of these provisions is to protect private individuals against the superior bargaining power of businesses. The Road Traffic Act 1988 prohibits exclusion of liability for negligence on the roads because it is compulsory to insure against such liability.

Tort liability may, in certain circumstances, be excluded or restricted by non-contractual agreement. For example, the liability of landowners to lawful visitors in respect of dangers on their land can be modified by a (non-contractual) 'notice' that was brought to the visitor's attention (*Ashdown v Williams* [1957] 1 QB 409). Liability for negligent misstatement may be modified by a (non-contractual) 'disclaimer' given to its addressee when the statement was made (*Hedley Byrne & Co Ltd v Heller & Partners Ltd* [1964] AC 465). The basis on which such non-contractual exclusions or limitations are effective is that if (as is generally the case) the landowner was free not to allow visitors onto the land, or if the person making the statement was free to remain silent, the landowner and the speaker respectively were also free to specify the conditions on which the freedom would be exercised in the harm-sufferer's favour. Under the Unfair Contract Terms Act non-contractual notices and disclaimers of negligence liability are subject to similar controls as apply to contractual provisions.

3. HARMFUL CONDUCT

We now turn to the other main element of the tort equation, as it were: the types of conduct from which tort law provides (and does not provide) protection. Just as tort law protects interests of both potential harm-sufferers and potential harm-doers, so it is also interested in conduct of both groups. Put differently, tort law plays a part in defining the freedom of action not only of potential harm-doers but also of potential harm-sufferers.

THE CONCEPT OF HARM AND THE REQUIREMENT OF DAMAGE

So far, tort law has been presented as about the 'doing and suffering of harm'. Now it is necessary to distinguish between 'harm' and 'damage'. In some cases, tort law provides protection against conduct only if it inflicts 'damage' on the harm-sufferer. The paradigm example is the tort of negligence. Here, 'damage' means physical or financial injury. In such cases, it is said, 'damage is the gist of the tort', and tort law protects interests only if damage to the harm-sufferer results from the conduct that interferes with the interest. In other cases, by contrast, tort law pro-tects interests regardless of whether the conduct that interferes with the interest causes any damage to the harm-sufferer. In such cases, it is said, the harm-causing conduct is 'actionable per se'. In other words, the conduct that interferes with the interest is considered 'harmful' even if it results in no damage to the harm-sufferer. What is action-able is the interference as such ('per se'), which is the 'gist' of the tort. Per se torts include misappropriation of land and chattels, and certain types of unauthorised exploitation of tangible and intangible property. Defamation is actionable per se in the sense that substantial damages for injury to reputation may be recovered even though the claimant does not have to (and could not) *prove* injury to reputation resulting from the defamatory publication.

In cases where damage is the gist of the harm-sufferer's complaint, tort will provide protection only if the harm-sufferer can prove that harm-doer's conduct *caused* damage to the harm-sufferer. Even in cases where harmful conduct is tortious per se, if the harm-sufferer claims to have suffered damage as a result of the tortious conduct (for instance, where the conduct is trespass to land and the claim is that the harm-doer not only entered the land but also damaged it), tort law will protect the harm-sufferer's interest in not being damaged only if the harm-sufferer can prove that the harm-doer's conduct caused the damage. Causation is a very complex and difficult area of tort law about which more will be said in Chapter 7. The basic point being made here is that conduct may be tortious and 'harmful' regardless of whether it causes any 'damage' to the harm-sufferer.

'CONDUCT'

In tort law, the word 'conduct' can refer both to acts and omissions or, more technically, 'misfeasance' and 'nonfeasance'. Both misfeasance and nonfeasance can be tortious. For instance, suppose A digs a hole in the unlit path leading from the gate of A's house to its front door. B falls into the hole at night and is injured. We would say that by the act of digging the hole, A caused B's damage—if A had not dug the hole, B would not have been injured. Suppose, alternatively, that the path had become pot-holed by the elements and C tripped in a hole at night. In this case we might say that A caused C's injury by omitting to repair the path: if A had kept the path in good repair, C would not have been injured. Put another way, we might say that whereas A caused B's injury, A failed to prevent C's injury.

In some cases in everyday life, we may judge a person less harshly for failing to prevent injury than for bringing it about. The thug who beats someone up may be judged more responsible for the person's injuries than the victim's (or the thug's) companion who makes no attempt to thwart the attack. But in other cases, we may react differently. A parent who harms their child by failing to feed it, even though they could afford to, is unlikely to be thought less culpable than a parent who causes the same harm by serving their child poisoned food. A passer-by who ignores an abandoned baby may be judged no less harshly than the parent who abandoned it. Just as omissions may attract as much moral censure as acts, so omissions may attract the same legal sanctions as acts.

In *Donoghue v Stevenson* [1932] AC 562, Lord Atkin said that the religious injunction to love your neighbour is translated by tort law into the principle that you must take care not to injure your neighbour. He did not mean by this that tort law does not impose liability for omissions. Indeed, the legal definition of negligent conduct is couched negatively in terms of a failure to take reasonable care; and a failure of reasonable care can consist either in doing something the reasonable person would not do or *not* doing something the reasonable person would do. As in everyday life, so in tort law: not doing can be as wrongful as doing.

Our attitude to omissions, in both law and life, depends on various factors including the status and situation of the person who fails to act, the costs of acting (both to the actor and to others), the status and situation of the person who would benefit from action, and the nature and size of that benefit. Perhaps all that can be said in general terms is that 'acts ... are often worse than omissions ... because they create the ... harms and risks of harm which omissions fail to remedy' (Honoré 1991, 33).

LEGAL STANDARDS OF CONDUCT

Tort law holds potential harm-doers to various different standards of conduct. In some cases, it protects interests only against deliberate, intentional conduct, while in others it also protects against negligent conduct, and in yet others, against conduct regardless of whether it is intentional or negligent. In this section, these various standards of conduct are explored in the abstract. In the next chapter, interests and conduct will be brought together to show the types of conduct against which tort law protects various interests.

Only Voluntary Conduct Can Be Tortious

Conduct can be tortious only if it was 'voluntary'. An involuntary action is a bodily movement over which the person had no control. If A physically overpowered B and used B as a missile to knock C to the ground, we would not say that B voluntarily knocked over C, or even (perhaps) that B knocked over C, but that A knocked over C using B. If A's car collides with B's car and causes it to knock over C, a pedestrian, we would not say that B voluntarily knocked over C, or even (perhaps) that B had knocked over C.

Suppose a person's lack of control is the result of some infirmity or incapacity resulting, for instance, from age, illness or intoxication. Tort law does not treat as involuntary bodily movements which are outside a person's control because of self-induced incapacity caused, for instance, by deliberate consumption of excessive amounts of alcohol or drugs. Lack of control will also be irrelevant if the person knew or ought to have known that they would or might not be able to control their movements. But a person who is unaware of suffering from a condition that may significantly impair bodily function may escape liability for harm caused as a result of unexpected onset of the condition (*Mansfield v Weetabix Ltd* [1998] 1 WLR 1263).

Doing something 'automatically' is not doing it involuntarily. 'Automaticity' is typically a result of repetition of tasks and the acquisition of skill. An experienced driver, for example, will do many things automatically or 'without thinking' or 'inadvertently' that a learner would do deliberately and attentively. Involuntary acts are uncontrollable whereas automatic acts are controllable but not consciously controlled. Far from being exempt from tort liability, automatic behaviour is frequently the very essence of tortious negligence. The competent driver is one who knows when it is necessary to pay attention and when doing things automatically will be safe.

Involuntariness must also be distinguished from incapacity. It is no answer to tort claim for the harm-doer to say that it was beyond their physical, mental or intellectual capacity to avoid committing a tort, even if the lack of capacity was not self-induced but was the result, for instance, of their genetic inheritance. The basic rule of tort law is that people are liable for failure to measure up to certain standards of behaviour even if reaching the required standard was beyond their capacities at the relevant time. Tort law does not exempt people from liability simply because they have the 'bad luck' of lacking the capacity, through no fault of their own, to measure up to the standards of conduct the law establishes. One explanation for this approach is that since everything a person does is affected to a greater or lesser extent by factors beyond their control ('luck'), exempting human beings from responsibility for any action which was not entirely within their control would destroy our sense of ourselves as rational, free agents, which is central to our individuality and feelings of achievement and self-worth. What's more, because our positive achievements in life are also more or less affected by factors beyond our control ('good luck'), it is considered unacceptable to take credit for them without being prepared to shoulder the blame for our failures, even though these are the result, more or less, of matters beyond our control ('bad luck'). Luck is an inescapable fact of life, and our ideas of personal responsibility largely ignore it. Only when a person's luck is abnormally or a typically good or bad are we likely to take it into account in allocating praise or blame to them.

Deliberation, Intention and Recklessness

There is an important distinction between 'voluntary' conduct and 'deliberate' conduct. All deliberate conduct is voluntary, but the converse is not true: conduct can be voluntary without being deliberate. Think of automatic or 'inadvertent' conduct, for instance. In tort law, conduct will sometimes be wrongful only if it is deliberate. For instance, inducing, encouraging, authorising or conspiring in the tortious conduct of another can be tortious only if it is deliberate. However, tort liability very often attaches to inadvertent conduct.

In tort law, there is also an important distinction between 'deliberate' conduct and 'intentional' conduct. Conduct is deliberate if it is done with deliberation: automatic conduct is not deliberate. Conduct is intentional if it is done with the intention (or 'aim') of causing a particular consequence. All intentional conduct is deliberate, but the converse is not true: not all deliberate conduct is intentional—that is, aimed at producing a particular result. A person may, for instance, deliberately hit another person and thereby cause the other's death without intending to kill that person. But a person who hits another, intending to kill the other thereby, could not claim to have hit without deliberation. Some torts (such as intimidation) can be committed only by conduct that is intentional in this sense—ie conduct that is not only deliberate but also aimed at having a particular effect (such as economic loss).

Recklessness is different from intention. Like intentional conduct, reckless conduct is necessarily deliberate. But to intend a consequence is to aim at producing it. To be reckless about a consequence is to *know* that one's action may produce it, without caring whether it will or not. A person who *ought to have known*, but did not actually know, of the riskiness of their conduct is not reckless. Although intention and recklessness are clearly distinguishable in theory, in tort law (as opposed to criminal law) they are generally treated as equivalent. A requirement in tort law, to prove (for instance) that D intended to injure C, can normally be satisfied by proof that D actually knew that their conduct might injure C but did it anyway. This is probably because both intentional and reckless conduct necessarily involve deliberation. Deliberate interference with another's interests is distinguishable from non-deliberate interference whether the outcome was intended or only the object of indifference. Harming a person by deliberate conduct indicates a fundamental lack of respect for that person's individuality.

Recklessness is also different from motive. To say that someone acted with indifference to consequences tells us nothing about why they did it. Motive is also different from intention. My intention in hitting someone may be to hurt them, but my motive for doing so may be to impress a

friend. The general rule in tort law is that the motive with which conduct was done is irrelevant to its tortiousness. If an interference with the
interests of another would not, as such, be tortious, the fact that it was
done out of a bad motive (with 'malice') would not make it tortious.
Conversely, tortious interference with the rights of another cannot be
excused by pleading a good motive.

Negligence

The concepts of deliberation, intention and recklessness refer to states
of mind. By contrast, in tort law 'negligence' refers not to a state of mind
but to failure to reach a certain standard of conduct. There is no necessary relationship between states of mind and negligence. Deliberate,
intentional and reckless conduct alike may attract tort liability for negligence if the conduct satisfies the definition of negligence by failing to
attain a certain standard. Negligence as failure to attain a standard must
be distinguished from the 'tort of negligence'. The tort of negligence is a
cause of action with three main elements: a duty of care, a breach of that
duty, and damage caused by the breach. As failure to attain a standard,
negligence corresponds to the second of these elements; and in this guise,
it is also an element of certain other torts, such as trespass to the person
causing personal injury.

Central to the concept of negligent conduct is the notion of 'risk'. Life
is full of risks. We are often prepared to accept a certain degree of risk
in order to secure the benefits that risky activities bring. Underlying the
concept of negligence is the assumption that a certain level of risk is an
inevitable and acceptable feature of human life. Negligence consists of
imposing an 'unreasonable' level of risk without taking reasonable precautions to prevent the risk materialising. The concept of negligence is
not about eliminating risk but about reducing it to an acceptable level by
taking reasonable precautions.

Several factors are taken into account in determining whether a person has been negligent in this sense. The first is whether the activity in
which the harm-doer was engaged was valuable enough (or whether its
benefits were great enough) to make the risks attached to it acceptable.
For instance, in one case the question was whether the risks attaching to
allowing left-hand drive vehicles on public roads were justified by the fact
that there was a shortage of ambulances (*Daborn v Bath Tramways Motor
Co Ltd* [1946] 2 All ER 333). Some activities, such as saving life and limb,

may be thought to justify the taking of risks which less valuable activities might not. But if an activity is considered not to be worth the risks attendant upon it, it would be negligent to engage in that activity.

Once it has been decided that it was not negligent to engage in the activity in the first place, the next question is whether the risk that has materialised was foreseeable. It is not negligent to fail to take precautions against an unforeseeable risk. A foreseeable risk is one which a person ought to have foreseen even if they were not consciously aware of the risk. In tort law, this point is made by saying that foreseeability is an 'objective', not a 'subjective' concept. The relevant question is not whether a person was actually ('subjectively') aware of a risk but whether they ought ('objectively') to have been aware of it.

What risks does tort law require people to foresee? Foresight is a function of knowledge, and the relevant questions are: at the time when it is alleged that the harm-doer ought to have taken precautions against the risk, did anyone have the knowledge required to foresee it? If so, ought the harm-doer have had that knowledge? The concept that tort law uses in answering this second question is that of 'reasonableness'. The harm-doer ought to have had the necessary knowledge if a reasonable person in the harm-doer's position would have had it.

Assuming that it was not negligent to engage in the activity in the first place, and that the risk was foreseeable, the next question is whether the harm-doer took reasonable care or precautions to eliminate the risk or reduce it to an acceptable level. This involves assessing the relative weight of three factors: the probability that the risk will materialise if no precautions are taken to prevent it, the likely seriousness of the adverse effect on the harm-sufferer if it does materialise, and the cost and difficulty of reducing the risk to a reasonable level. In light of these factors, the question is whether the harm-doer acted reasonably in the face of the risk, in the way the reasonable person would.

In theory, at least, the probability and likely seriousness of many risks could be ascertained with some degree of statistical precision, as could the cost of elimination or reasonable reduction. In practice, however, many risks are unquantifiable or their magnitude is contested; and there may frequently be irresolvable disagreement about the cost of elimination or reasonable reduction. Even if reasonably precise and agreed mathematical values could be given to the three factors of probability, seriousness and cost, their relative weight and the ultimate question of acceptability is inevitably a matter of judgment. Like decisions about the value of activities, decisions about the acceptability of risks are ultimately based on the decision-maker's view of what constitutes the good society. Also, although the three factors listed above represent the formal structure of reasoning about reasonable care, in practice the three factors are often not explicitly referred to and the court will simply make a global judgment about reasonable care.

Whether any precautions taken were reasonable is judged in the light of all the circumstances, as a 'question of fact'. However, there are also certain relevant legal (ie fixed) principles which apply to all cases of negligence. First, tort law explicitly recognises two degrees of unreasonableness—let's call them 'ordinary unreasonableness' and 'extraordinary unreasonableness'. Ordinarily unreasonable conduct is conduct which, in the court's view, would be thought unreasonable by the generality of people suitably qualified to have an opinion on the matter, even if some of those people would think it reasonable. Extraordinarily unreasonable conduct is conduct which, in the court's view, would be thought unreasonable by all those suitably qualified to have an opinion on the matter: if a suitably qualified body of opinion, however small, would think the conduct reasonable, it would not be extraordinarily unreasonable.

Normally, conduct will fail the test of reasonableness if it is ordinarily unreasonable. However, in certain cases, conduct will fail the test of reasonableness only if it is extraordinarily unreasonable. The two main categories of case in which the extraordinarily unreasonable test applies are claims against medical practitioners (and, perhaps, members of the other long-established professions, such as lawyers) (*Bolam v Friern Hospital Management Committee* [1957] 1 WLR 582), and certain actions against public authorities such as county councils. Such leniency to doctors and other professionals is designed to give them freedom to experiment with unorthodox but potentially beneficial practices. It is also based on a belief that being held liable for negligence is likely to have a particularly damaging effect on the reputation and livelihood of professionals. This approach is highly controversial. The leniency to public authorities is based on a desire not to overburden the public purse with orders to pay damages, and the idea that government needs considerable freedom to act (or to refrain from action) in the public interest, even if such conduct injures individual citizens.

In judging whether a person's conduct was reasonable, various circumstances are normally ignored (*Nettleship v Weston* [1971] 2 QB 691). The first is the harm-doer's degree of relevant skill or experience with the harm-causing activity. The pragmatic justification for this rule is that it would be exceedingly difficult to operate a system of standards of care that varied according to individual skill and experience. This might seem harsh on harm-doers; but as between the two parties, it is considered fair that the risk of lack of skill or experience should rest on the harm-doer rather than the harm-sufferer, especially since any failure by the harm-sufferer to take reasonable care of their own interests can be treated as 'contributory negligence' or 'voluntary assumption of risk', which are defences discussed below.

Second, age is ignored unless the person was too young yet to have developed the mental and social skills, imparted by education and experience, necessary to have an adult appreciation of risk (*McHale v Watson* (1966) 115 CLR 199). This rule is based on a unitary conception of adulthood which, while perhaps scientifically contestable, is considered ethically sound. As far as the law is concerned, adults who cannot take reasonable precautions should not engage in risky activities; but if they do, they cannot complain if they are required to bear the consequences. Third, the harm-doer's financial resources and physical and mental abilities are also usually ignored. The value-judgement underlying this rule is similar: that people ought to acknowledge their limitations and mould their activities accordingly. Those who cannot afford, or are not able, to take necessary precautions against the risks of an activity should not engage in the activity; but if they do, they cannot complain if they are required to bear the consequences. In two situations, however, tort law does take account of the harm-doer's resources and abilities, namely, when a landowner is sued for injury suffered by a trespasser arising out of some danger on the land, and where a landowner is sued for damage suffered by a neighbour as a result of neglect by the landowner of the state of the land (*Goldman v Hargrave* [1967] 1 AC 645). In these two contexts, landowners are not expected to take precautions beyond their resources. The first of these exceptions is usually justified on the basis that trespassers are, in some sense, undeserving; and the second rests on an old idea that landowners should be free to do what they want with their land, even to the point of letting it deteriorate.

Conduct Neither Intentional Nor Negligent

Tort law sometimes classifies as wrongful conduct that was not intentional, reckless, negligent or, even, deliberate, provided it was voluntary.

Tort liability for such conduct is called 'strict'. Tort law recognises several quite distinct types of strict liability. First, strict liability may attach to voluntarily doing a specified act, most notably interference with or exploitation of another's property without their consent or legal justification. For example, a person can be liable for taking another's property and treating it as their own even if they did not know and had no reason to know that the property was not theirs (as when a person is duped into buying a stolen car), and even if they did not deliberately take it (as when a person inadvertently takes a pen from a customer desk in a bank). This form of strict liability expresses the very high value put on real and personal property, and the importance attached to making it easy for people to recover their property by recourse to law and discouraging possibly violent self-help. The institution of private property is fundamental to our society, and a powerful way of expressing the distinction between 'what is mine and what is yours' is through such a rule of strict liability.

This form of strict liability is also found in the law of defamation. The basic rule (subject to limited qualifications) is that a person can be liable for defamation even if they did not know and had no reason to suspect that they were publishing a defamatory statement, or even that the defamed person existed. Once again, strict liability here expresses the very high value put on reputation, although many would question this valuation now that freedom of expression is thought so important. Indeed, in light of the fact that tort liability for inflicting personal injury or property damage is typically not strict, giving such strong protection to property and reputation may seem out of touch with contemporary values.

A second type of strict liability is called 'vicarious liability'. Vicarious liability is liability for the tortious conduct of another, and it is imposed on the basis that the person vicariously liable is in a certain relationship with the harm-doer. The main relationship which attracts vicarious liability is that of employer and employee—employers are vicariously liable for tortious conduct of their employees, committed in the course of their employment. The employer may be vicariously liable even if the employer did not intend the tortious conduct to be committed; was not negligent in letting it happen and did not know and could not have known that it was happening; and even if the employer had forbidden the conduct.

The law of vicarious liability is complex, and this complexity has defeated many attempts to justify it. Two types of argument can be mentioned here. The first seeks to find a justification in some principle of personal responsibility. For instance, it has been suggested that those who engage in activities for profit should bear the costs of tortious conduct arising out of that activity (Stapleton 1994a, chapter 8). The second type of argument seeks to justify vicarious liability in terms of 'efficient loss distribution'. Arguments of this type rest on the assumption that an important use of tort law is to compensate victims of tortious conduct. Vicarious liability furthers this aim by increasing the chance that the victim will be compensated: in general, employers are likely to be in a better position than employees to pay tort damages or to insure against tort liability. A full assessment of these contrasting approaches would require a detailed exposition of the law of vicarious liability and a close examination of the arguments, which is not possible here.

A third type of strict liability in tort law is based on the idea of risk creation. This form of strict liability, unlike the first two, applies to situations in which the harm-doer's risky conduct causes damage to the harm-sufferer. The liability is strict because the harm-doer can be liable even without intending to cause damage to the harm-sufferer, without recklessly ignoring the risk of damage, and without being negligent in creating the risk. This third type of strict liability is very rare in tort law, especially in judge-made tort law. Under the so-called 'rule in *Rylands v Fletcher*' a landowner can be held liable for the escape from the land of things likely to cause damage if they escape, and which the landowner has accumulated on the land for their own purposes and in the course of a 'non-natural' use of the land. On the face of it, this principle looks like a principle of strict liability: the risky activity is accumulation of dangerous things for a non-natural purpose, and the principle contains no requirement of intention, recklessness or negligence. However, the rule has been interpreted in such a way as to weaken its claim to be a rule of strict liability. The term 'non-natural' has been given a meaning close to 'negligent'; there can be liability under the rule only in relation to 'foreseeable' damage; and although the harm-sufferer need not prove that the escape was the result of either deliberate or negligent conduct by the landowner, the landowner will not be liable if the escape can be shown to have been the result of a natural event or human conduct that was not foreseeable by the harm-doer.

The rarity of this third form of strict liability in tort law may be explained by an idea that there should be 'no legal liability in tort without fault'. This adage rests, perhaps, on an assumption that in daily

life people are not held responsible for outcomes that they did not intend
and that they could not have avoided with reasonable care. However, this
assumption is contestable. It has been argued, for instance, that we are
sometimes prepared to hold a person responsible for an outcome that
the person caused but that they neither intended nor could have avoided,
provided the person is of 'full age and capacity', so to speak (Honoré
1988). The basic idea of 'outcome responsibility' is that risk-taking is part
of ordinary human life, and that when we take risks, sometimes things
turn out well and sometimes they turn out badly. Since we take the benefit when things turn out well, we may be expected also to take responsibility when things turn out badly, even if we could have done nothing
to prevent the bad outcome. This argument by itself does not, of course,
tell us when outcome responsibility, as opposed to responsibility only for
fault, is appropriate.

Some people have found problematic not only strict liability for damage but also negligence liability. The test of reasonableness in negligence
is objective. Reasonable precautions are precautions that the reasonable
person would have taken regardless of whether they are precautions that
the person whose conduct is under scrutiny *could* have taken. Under this
test, people may be held liable in negligence for doing things that
they could not personally have avoided doing at the relevant time and
for failing to do things that they could not personally have done at the
relevant time, not because of any 'fault' on their part but just because
they had the 'bad luck' to be born lacking the skill or capacity needed to
meet the standard of conduct which the law considers to be reasonable.
However, it might be argued that because the good or bad luck of being
born with certain characteristics is an ineradicable feature of the human
condition, we must all do what we can to correct deficiencies in our per-
sonalities and capacities that are apt to produce wrongful conduct. We
should also (it might be thought) avoid tasks that we know or ought to
realise we are not capable of performing without harming others. Arguments like this may justify holding people responsible for conduct that
they could not have avoided.

We may even blame people for conduct attributable to incorrigible
personal characteristics or forgivable ignorance of their limitations.
Everything we do (or fail to do) is affected to a greater or lesser extent
by 'lucky' factors beyond our control, including our personal endowments. If people could disclaim responsibility for their conduct simply by pointing to the role of luck in their endowments and capacities,

the whole concept of personal responsibility, on which our sense of ourselves and others as rational and free agents depends, would dissolve.
It is only when a person's natural endowments fall below a minimum
level that we are prepared to allow luck to affect our judgements about
the person's responsibility for their conduct. Just as it is often acceptable
for people to claim personal credit for conduct that is partly a product
of their good luck in having a certain personality and certain capacities,
so people must often accept responsibility for conduct that is partly a
product of bad luck in having a certain personality and certain capacities.

Tort law, then, is a complex mixture of principles of personal responsibility for conduct (whether intentional, reckless or negligent) and personal responsibility for outcomes (strict liability). Different ideas underlie
these two forms of responsibility. Responsibility for conduct rests on
ideas about how we ought to behave in going about our various activities, while responsibility for outcomes rests on the idea that we should
compensate for adverse consequences of our risky activities. Viewed in
this way, tort liability for outcomes is a sort of tax on activities that attract
such liability rather than a penalty for engaging in them. Responsibility
for conduct, by contrast, implies disapproval of the liability-attracting
conduct that does not attach merely to liability for outcomes.

SELF-HARMING CONDUCT

As we have already noted, tort law is concerned with the conduct of
harm-sufferers as well as harm-doers. This concern partly finds expression in certain defences to tort liability that relate to the conduct of the
harm-sufferer.

Contributory Negligence

Negligent conduct on the part of the harm-sufferer ('contributory
negligence') may provide an answer to a tort claim in the sense of justifying a reduction in the damages payable to the claimant. Contributory negligence consists of failure to take care for one's own interests;
and it may be intentional (*Corr v IBC Vehicles Ltd* [2008] 1 AC 884).
The concept of unreasonable conduct underlying contributory negligence
is essentially similar to that underlying liability-attracting negligence.
For instance, contributory negligence is an objective concept depending
on what the reasonable person would have done in the harm-sufferer's

position. However, the law allows people to take less care for their own interests than it requires people to take for the interests of others. In technical terms, this means that in judging the reasonableness of the precautions a person takes to protect their own interests, the law makes more allowance for age, resources, and physical and mental capacity than in the case of liability-attracting negligence.

Is contributory negligence an answer to a claim based on intention/recklessness? The Law Reform (Contributory Negligence) Act 1945, which created the defence, does not resolve this issue. If a person intends to harm another, it may not seem fair to allow that person to argue that the victim did not take sufficient care to protect himself or herself from being harmed. The idea that a person might have 'deserved what they got' because they took insufficient precautions to avoid it may be acceptable as a judgment of the harm-sufferer relative to other (hypothetical) harm-sufferers. But the important question concerns the relative positions of the harm-sufferer and the harm-doer.

So far as strict liability is concerned, it might be argued that if fault is irrelevant to the issue of whether the harm-doer's conduct attracts liability, it should also be irrelevant to the issue of whether the harm-sufferer's conduct gives rise to a defence. However, the strength of this argument may depend, in part, on the sort of strict liability in issue. In relation to strict liability for outcomes (the third type of strict liability discussed earlier), we might think it fair both to require potential harm-sufferers to take reasonable care for their own safety, and also not to allow harm-doers to plead as a defence the negligence of anyone other than the harm-sufferer. This sort of approach is reflected in the fact that statutes which impose outcome-based strict liability not infrequently also allow contributory negligence to be pleaded as a defence. It might also seem fair that a defendant who is vicariously liable should be allowed to take advantage of a defence of contributory negligence which was available to the harm-doer. By contrast, in the case of the type of strict liability the primary role of which is to protect property rights (and analogous interests, such as reputation), the law has consistently followed the principle that people should not be expected to take care of their own property: the fact that I am careless of my property may make me an unworthy owner, but it does not make the property any less mine.

The principle that people should take reasonable care for themselves as well as for others finds expression in tort law not only in the defence of contributory negligence but also in rules about when tort liability can arise in the first place. Such rules figure prominently in the law governing liability for purely economic loss. For instance, liability for financial loss, suffered as a result of relying on the accuracy of a statement made by the harm-doer to the harm-sufferer, will arise only if it was reasonable for the harm-sufferer to rely on the statement as being accurate (*Hedley Byrne v Heller* [1964] AC 465).

Consent

In principle, a person cannot complain in tort about conduct to which they have consented. For example, there can be no liability for trespass to land if the owner consented to the entry; and it is a defence to an action for defamation that the person to whom the statement refers consented to its publication. Consent is a subjective concept: the relevant question is not whether the reasonable person would have consented but whether the victim in fact consented. However, consent will provide a defence only if the harm-sufferer was not 'forced' by the harm-doer to consent. The test of whether consent was forced is ultimately an objective one: did the victim consent to the tort because the defendant threatened that if (s)he did not, (s)he would suffer some negative consequence which the court thinks it would not be reasonable to expect the victim to accept as the price of avoiding the tort?

In relation to negligence, the defence of consent is usually expressed in terms of the Latin maxim '*volenti non fit injuria*' or its English translation 'voluntary assumption of risk'. It has often been argued that the notion of consent-in-advance is inconsistent with the legal concept of negligence because it is impossible fully to appreciate in advance the risks attendant upon lack of reasonable care. This argument depends partly on the incorrect assumption that legal negligence implies inadvertence: in cases where negligence liability attaches to deliberate conduct, there is no logical difficulty in the idea of prospective consent. If I freely allow myself to be driven at night in a car which the driver has told me has no lights, I may be said to have voluntarily assumed the risk of being injured in an accident attributable to absence of lights. If I freely agree to be a passenger in an aircraft piloted by a person whom I know to have consumed 20 units of alcohol in a few hours, I may be said to have voluntarily assumed the risk of being injured in an accident attributable to the pilot's drunkenness (*Morris v Murray* [1991] 2 QB 6). In such cases I may be said, by my conduct, to have consented to a lack of reasonable care on the part of another.

Illegality

Suppose the harm-sufferer was acting illegally (typically in breach of the criminal law) at the time of the harm-doer's tortious conduct—a not uncommon occurrence. For instance, many victims of road accidents are in breach of traffic regulations at the time the accident occurs. Such illegal conduct on the part of the victim might amount to contributory negligence. But independently of that, the issue is whether the fact that the victim was acting illegally provides the harm-doer with a defence. On the one hand, it might be thought that a person who acts illegally hardly deserves much sympathy from the law. On the other hand, many technically illegal acts might not be thought very culpable. Moreover, suppose the illegal behaviour in no way contributed to the accident or to the harm-sufferer's damage; should the mere fact that a harm-sufferer was acting illegally affect their rights under tort law?

It seems that tort law gives harm-doers a defence of illegality only if the harm-sufferer's illegal conduct contributed in some significant way to bringing about the situation for which the harm-doer is held responsible. Tort law is not concerned with sanctioning conduct as such. This is the province of the criminal law, the focus of which is on punishment. Criminal law may sanction conduct that creates risks of adverse outcomes, even if the risk never materialises. Tort law, by contrast, will only sanction risky conduct if the risk materialises. The primary concern of tort law is not to punish risky conduct but to make good the adverse effects of risky conduct. Of course, requiring someone to make good the adverse consequences of their risky conduct may be seen as a form of punishment for that conduct; and in fact, criminal courts have powers to award compensation to victims of crimes, and civil courts have limited powers to impose 'punishments' on tortfeasors. Nevertheless, the focus of tort law and criminal law are different: criminal law is primarily concerned with risky conduct as such, whereas tort law is concerned with the adverse consequences of risky conduct. An unsuccessful attempt to commit a crime may be a crime. There is no such thing as an 'attempted tort'. The approach of the law in this respect reflects the idea that whereas the prime function that the criminal law can fulfil is punishment, the prime function of tort law is the protection and vindication of individuals' interests, typically by compensating for damage suffered. As far as the law is concerned, this function would be unacceptably compromised if 'contributory illegality' on the part of the harm-sufferer, however trivial, provided a defence.

5

Torts Repackaged

KI 3: Each tort has two main elements:

(1) conduct that is classified by tort law as wrongful
and
(2) one or more interests with which that conduct has interfered in ways specified by tort law

In the previous chapter, a tort was unpacked into two separate elements: protected interests and harmful conduct. Not all torts, and not all protected interests, were mentioned, but the analysis is equally applicable to any and every tort. In this chapter we put the pieces back together again by joining up the two elements to show the sorts of conduct against which tort law protects interests. This is a complex task, and to do it in full detail would require a much longer treatment. The aim here will be to produce a line-drawing rather than a fully worked-up portrait. Because there are two elements to fit into the picture, the first question is how to organise the discussion? Here, this is done in terms of protected interests rather than harmful conduct. Tort claims are, of course, always initiated by harm-sufferers. In *practical* terms, tort law is first and foremost a resource that people can utilise to protect and further their interests.

1. INTERESTS IN ONE'S PERSON

INTERESTS IN BODY AND MIND

Personal health and safety lie at the core of tort law. Contract law also protects this interest; but in both theory and practice, 'personal injury claims' based on contract are of marginal importance in the total picture of contract law. Criminal law is also much concerned with personal health and safety; and in practice, the conduct which forms the basis of very many tort claims for personal injuries is criminal as well as tortious. However, in practice, leaving aside traffic offences, very little criminal behaviour causing personal injuries ever becomes the subject of a tort claim.

As we have seen, in tort law there is an important difference between bodily injury and mental injury. Infliction of bodily injury may be tortious if it is inflicted intentionally, recklessly or negligently and (often) regardless of whether the harmful conduct directly caused the injury or merely failed to prevent it. Although tort law recognises no 'duty to rescue' in the narrow sense of a duty to take difficult, costly or risky steps to prevent a complete stranger suffering personal injury, in practice there are many types of case in which tort law imposes liability for failures of physical protection.

In the 'tort of negligence' the device used, to identify when liability for failure to prevent harm may arise, is the 'duty of care'. This device deserves some explanation because most personal injury tort claims are based on the tort of negligence. This tort has three elements: duty of care; breach of duty; and damage, 'not too remote in law', caused by the breach of duty. There can be no liability in the tort of negligence unless the harm-doer owed a duty of care to the harm-sufferer and committed a breach of that duty, thereby causing damage to the harm-sufferer. The discussion of negligent conduct in Chapter 4 above was largely a discussion of the second element. The first, duty of care, element of the tort of negligence is used to refine and give more detailed content to the concepts of protected interests and harmful conduct.

The classic general statement about when a duty of care is owed is the 'neighbour principle' enunciated by Lord Atkin in *Donoghue v Stevenson* [1932] AC 562, at 580: everyone owes a duty of care to their neighbours. A neighbour is someone you ought to foresee as likely to suffer harm if you are negligent. The neighbour principle has since been fleshed out by a three-stage test under which a duty of care will be owed if the harm-doer ought to have foreseen injury to harm-sufferer, there was a 'sufficient relationship of proximity' between the harm-doer and the harm-sufferer, and it would be 'fair, just and reasonable' to impose a duty of care (*Caparo Industries Plc v Dickman* [1990] 2 AC 605). The first element (foreseeability) is more-or-less redundant because foreseeability of risk is central to the concept of negligent conduct. The other two elements (proximity, and justice and reasonableness) are labels attached to the various grounds on which the courts think it right to restrict the scope of liability for negligently-caused injury. The duty of care concept operates negatively to impose limits on the potentially enormous breadth of application of the principle that people ought to be legally liable for negligently-caused injury.

To return to the distinction between acts and omissions that prompted this digression: in tort law omissions are, in principle, less likely than acts to be tortious. In general, tort law imposes a duty to take care not to cause personal injury by a negligent act unless some countervailing reason not to recognise a duty can be found. In relation to negligent omissions, the law starts from the other end and looks for some justification for imposing a duty of care. Tort law recognises many duties to take reasonable care to prevent physical injury. For example, employers owe duties 'of positive action' to protect the health and safety of their workers; and occupiers of land owe duties of positive action to visitors coming onto the land. There may be no duty to protect or rescue a complete stranger from danger, particularly if doing so would be costly or dangerous, but doctors have duties of physical protection towards their patients, as do parents towards their children, school authorities towards their pupils, and prison authorities towards prisoners. A surveyor or architect employed to certify the safety of a building would also owe a duty of positive action to someone injured by the building, whether the employer or not. A person who creates a dangerous situation may be under a duty to protect or rescue a person who falls into the danger, even if that person is a stranger.

One important question to which the law currently gives no clear answer is whether a public regulatory body (as opposed to a private individual) charged with the function of monitoring and enforcing compliance with health and safety regulations and standards by citizens, would owe a duty, to take care in monitoring and enforcement, to a person for whose benefit the regulations and standards existed and who was injured as a result of non-compliance with them. The question here is whether the regulatory body's responsibility should be treated as outweighed by the wrongful conduct of the person subject to regulation. It is the latter, we might say, who was 'primarily responsible' for the injuries; the former was only 'secondarily responsible'. It is not obvious, we might think, that the regulator should be totally free of liability simply on the ground of being only secondarily responsible; especially since the law-breaker could also be held liable and since, as between the two, the law-breaker would be held liable to pay more of the damages than the regulator. In practice, however, if regulators owed duties of care to individual beneficiaries of regulatory schemes, they would present very attractive targets for tort actions because their liabilities are ultimately underwritten by public funds (tax revenue). It might also prove very difficult for a regulatory body held liable in tort successfully to offload part of the burden of liability on to the law-breaker even though the law-breaker may well have been, in some sense, much more responsible for what happened than the regulator.

The duty of care concept is also used to regulate the scope of liability for mental injuries, which was discussed in Chapter 4.

So much for negligence. Strict tort liability for interference with interests in body and mind is exceptional. In practice, the most important head of strict tort liability is vicarious liability. However, vicarious 'liability' is not 'a tort' because it arises regardless of whether the person liable did anything wrong. Liability that is negligence-based in theory may be strict in practice if the harm-doer bears the burden of disproving negligence under the so-called doctrine of *res ipsa loquitur* (loosely translatable as: this sort of thing does not normally happen without negligence). It is typically very difficult to prove a negative proposition such as that the harm-doer did not do anything negligent. The combination of vicarious liability and reversal of the burden of proving negligence can produce a particularly powerful form of strict liability. For instance, if a patient undergoes surgery to restore movement to a stiff finger and ends up with two stiff fingers, the hospital may be liable even if it cannot be proved that any member of the theatre staff was negligent, simply on the basis that this sort of thing does not normally happen without negligence, and the hospital cannot prove that none of the staff was negligent (*Cassidy v Ministry of Health* [1951] 2 KB 343).

Why is strict liability exceptional and 'fault' (in the sense of intention, recklessness or negligence) such a pervasive feature of tort liability for personal injuries? In general terms, this question is extremely difficult to answer. It is sometimes argued that fault-based liability is 'fair' and that strict liability is not. On this basis, however, large parts of the private law of obligations—notably liability for breach of contract—would have to be condemned as unfair; and as we saw in Chapter 4, a case can be made in favour of strict liability in tort law. Criticisms of strict liability are more often based on perceived anomalies generated by applying different standards of liability to essentially similar types of case than on objections

to strict liability as such. Why, for instance, are people prepared to con-
template strict liability for injuries caused by defective products but not
for injuries caused by defective services (Stapleton 1994a, 323ff)?

The fact that tort liability for personal injuries is typically fault-based
means that contributory negligence is a very important defence to tort
claims for interference with interests in mind and body. But even in cases
where liability for personal injuries is, in some sense, strict (as in relation to defective products under the Consumer Protection Act 1987),
contributory negligence is usually available as a defence. The defence of
assumption of risk also finds its most important (though small) area of
operation in personal injury claims.

DIGNITARY INTERESTS

The dignitary interest best protected by tort law is reputation. Reputation
is treated as analogous to property, and liability for damage to reputation is very strict. The only thing a claimant in a defamation action has
to establish to get the action off the ground is that a statement defamatory of the claimant was communicated ('published'), by the maker
of the statement or someone else, to a person other than the claimant.
The defamed person does not have to prove that the publication resulted
in damage to reputation; any and every person who publishes a defamatory statement has prima facie committed a tort. In the typical case,
publication will be deliberate; but liability may arise for inadvertent
publication. The maker of a defamatory statement may be liable for publication by another if the maker is vicariously liable for the torts of the
other, or authorised the publication, or intended or ought to have foreseen that publication.

It is a defence (called 'justification') to prove that the defamatory statement was a reasonable inference from substantially true facts. A person
cannot complain if the truth causes them harm. The defendant has a
defence (of 'fair comment') if it can be proved that the statement was an
expression of opinion, that it was an honestly believed (even if unreasonable) inference from substantially true facts, and that it concerned a 'matter of public interest'. This defence will not succeed if the defamer acted
out of what the law regards as an improper motive (with 'malice', for some
reason other than contributing to public debate); but it is the defamed
who must prove improper motive. 'Absolute privilege' protects statements made in the course of parliamentary and judicial proceedings; and

qualified privilege protects statements made in situations where the maker and the recipient have what the law considers to be legitimate interests in the making and receiving of the statement. Qualified privilege can be 'defeated' if the defamed can prove malice in the making of the statement (lack of honest belief in the truth of the statement, or making the statement for a purpose other than that which the privilege protects); but absolute privilege cannot. The defence of justification rests on the simple principle that no one deserves to have or to retain a good reputation based on falsehood. The other defences are designed to protect the interest of citizens in knowing things that are of legitimate interest to them as members of society.

Generally, it is no defence to a claim in defamation that the defamer took reasonable care not to injure the reputation of the defamed. There are two major qualifications to the general rule. One is that if the person sued did not make the statement but only disseminated it, there will be no liability if the disseminator did not know that the statement was defamatory and took reasonable care not to publish a defamatory statement (Defamation Act 1996, section 1). Second, if the person sued took reasonable care not to defame, and if they make an 'offer of amends' that the defamed refuses to accept, the person sued can plead the making of the offer as a defence to the claim (Defamation Act 1996, sections 2–4). However, the effect of this second qualification is simply to make it easier for an 'innocent defendant' to settle the claim out of court. The section assumes that the 'innocent' defendant has committed tortious defamation.

The strictness of liability for defamation is controversial because it represents a very significant intrusion on individual freedom of speech. In modern society, freedom of speech and information is considered a 'fundamental human right'. In traditional English tort law, by contrast, reputation is more highly prized than freedom of speech and information, and such protections for the latter as are recognised are embodied in defences to a claim for defamation rather than in the definition of the wrong of defamation. Many believe that the law of defamation unduly protects public figures, such as politicians, from proper scrutiny by the press who, in an open society, perform a pivotal 'quasi-constitutional' role in maintaining the free flow of socially important information and views. In some jurisdictions (in the US, for instance) the standard of liability in defamation actions brought by public figures is much less strict than in England (*Reynolds v Times Newspapers Ltd* [2001] 2 AC 127). By contrast, some would argue that strict defamation laws are needed to protect people, who have not chosen to put themselves into the limelight, from the attentions of less scrupulous sections of the press. Those who argue along such lines are also usually concerned that the law gives insufficient protection to people's privacy. In fact (as we have already noted), although there is no tort of 'breach of privacy', various other torts (such as trespass) can be used to protect aspects of privacy.

CIVIL AND POLITICAL INTERESTS

The only such interest to which tort law gives direct and significant protection (through the tort of wrongful or false imprisonment) is personal liberty. Deprivation of liberty against a person's will is typically the result of deliberate restriction of movement, but inadvertent restriction can also attract liability. In practice, the most important defence to a claim for deprivation of liberty is legal authority. The common (ie judge-made) law authorises detention in the name of preserving the peace, and an important ground of statutory authority is law enforcement. There are also some statutory powers to detain people on medical grounds. In the contexts of public order and law enforcement, the main basis of authorisation (apart from court orders in the form of warrants for arrest or orders for imprisonment) is reasonable suspicion that a ground for detention exists. The effect of the reasonable suspicion test is to inject an element of fault into a head of liability to which fault is essentially irrelevant: the detainer must take reasonable steps to ensure that the suspicion that a ground of detention exists is well-founded. In relation to the police, suspicion will only be unreasonable if no reasonable police officer would have had a suspicion in the circumstances (*Holgate-Mohammed v Duke* [1984] AC 437).

2. PROPERTY INTERESTS

REAL PROPERTY

As we saw in Chapter 4, in the common law of torts, liability for misappropriation and unauthorised exploitation of real property is typically strict in the sense that there can be liability even if the harm-doer acted inadvertently and neither knew nor ought reasonably to have known that the property was the harm-sufferer's. It is no defence that the harm-sufferer failed to take reasonable care to protect the property from the intruders. Misappropriation of real property is actionable per se, without proof of financial or physical damage.

The rationale for these rules is that in English law, tort performs in relation to property what might be called a 'vindicatory' function or, in other words, the function of marking the boundary between 'what is mine and what is yours'. What is mine is no less mine because I do not take care of it or because you had no reason to know it was mine. In this respect, tort law is much more concerned with the nature of the protected interest than with the nature of the interfering conduct.

More than one person may have property rights in one and the same piece of property at the same time. Thus, tort law provides remedies not only to dispossessed owners but also to dispossessed tenants. The owner is protected not only against 'squatters' but also against 'overstaying' tenants. Tenants are protected not only against dispossession by third parties but also against dispossession by the owner during the period of the tenancy. The common law drew a sharp distinction between the rights of tenants (who have a property interest in the rented premises) and 'licensees' (who have only a contractual interest in the premises). As we have seen, on the whole, the common law of tort gives no protection to merely contractual interests in real property. However, residential licensees now enjoy, by statute, many of the protections accorded to tenants against the owner; but their position vis-a-vis third parties is still precarious.

When we come to liability for interference with the use and enjoyment of land, the legal picture is rather different. Two heads of tort liability are important here—trespass and nuisance. In this context, trespass is used primarily to deal with unwanted entrants. Not all unwanted intrusions are necessarily tortious—for instance, the owner is assumed (in the absence of contrary indication) to be willing to allow people, under normal circumstances, to enter the land to get to the front door of a dwelling; and it is not an actionable trespass to fly in an aircraft over someone's land at a normal height even though, in theory, ownership of land carries with it ownership of the airspace above it (*Bernstein v Skyviews & General Ltd* [1978] QB 479). However, liability for unauthorised entry is strict and actionable per se: the law gives strong protection to the owner's right to control entry.

Whereas trespass deals with unreasonable interference with the use and enjoyment of land by entry, nuisance deals with interference by things done off the land. The requirement of unreasonableness is practically equivalent to a requirement of negligence: the interference with use and enjoyment must have been foreseeable, and it must be greater than it is reasonable to expect the harm-sufferer to put up with. The philosophy of the law of nuisance is mutual tolerance: 'live and let live'. The likely cost of preventing the interference and the social value of interfering activity are relevant to judging reasonableness.

In the nineteenth century, the law of nuisance played an important role in resolving conflicts between competing uses of land, particularly industrial and non-industrial. In the twentieth century this function was largely taken over by the statutory land-use planning system, which aims in part to prevent incompatible, contiguous uses of land. However, the law of nuisance still operates at the margins of the planning system to deal particularly with problems generated by the day-to-day use of land with which the planning system is not directly concerned, or with 'planning mistakes'. In one case, for instance, houses for which planning permission had been obtained were located so close to a playing field that they became targets for stray cricket balls (*Miller v Jackson* [1977] QB 966). In another, a shipping terminal, for which planning permission had been obtained, generated far more noise and traffic than local residents had anticipated (*Allen v Gulf Oil Refining Ltd* [1981] AC 1001). The law says that if a use of land has been authorised by statute, this provides an answer to a tort claim even if the use causes a nuisance. By contrast, the mere fact that planning permission (administrative authorisation) has been obtained for a particular use does not prevent that use being an actionable nuisance. These rules illustrate that tort law is a complex amalgam of judge-made and statutory rules.

Finally, the basic standard of liability for physical damage to, or the destruction or loss of, real property is fault—intention or, more commonly, negligence. The few instances of strict liability are statutory.

CHATTELS

The basic pattern of liability rules in this context is the same as that which applies to real property: strict liability for misappropriation and unauthorised exploitation, and fault-based liability for interference with use and enjoyment, and for physical damage.

INTANGIBLE PROPERTY

This is not the place to examine in detail the rules about infringement of the various intellectual property rights. Except in a few cases where action cannot amount to an infringement of an intellectual property right unless the infringer knew or ought to have known of the harm-sufferer's rights, liability for infringement (exploitation) of statutory intellectual property rights is strict. Common-law (ie non-statutory) liability in the tort of passing-off for harm suffered as a result of exploitation of goodwill is quite strict.

Damage to goodwill without exploitation is actionable under the head of 'malicious (or 'injurious') falsehood'. This is a form of defamation involving false statements reflecting on someone's business or commercial reputation as opposed to their personal reputation. However, liability depends on proof that the harm-doer acted 'maliciously', which means either that they did not honestly believe that the false statement was true, or acted out of some improper motive, that is some motive other than the protection of their own legitimate interests. The typical case of malicious falsehood arises as between business competitors, and this probably explains why malice must be proved: otherwise healthy competition might be unduly impeded. In the typical case, the tort is actionable per se: damage to business reputation need not be proved.

TORT LAW AND THE PROTECTION OF PROPERTY INTERESTS

The foregoing account shows how tort law protects four important incidents of property: the right to possess, the right to control use and to exploit, the right to enjoy, and the right that property should not be damaged, destroyed or lost. The two most distinctive characteristics of tortious protection of property interests are actionability per se and strict liability. As we have seen, however, neither characteristic is universal. Damage is often the gist of tort actions arising out of interference with property interests; and where damage is the gist of the action, the standard of liability is usually negligence or even malice, as in the tort of injurious falsehood. Most types of actionable interference with property rights can only be committed by positive acts, and not by omissions. This may be explained as a trade-off against strict liability and actionability per se.

The complexity of tort law in this area reflects the complexity of our concept of property and of the numerous social functions that property performs. Tort law plays an important part not only in protecting people's interests in property but also in shaping and defining the social roles of property: property is valuable not only as a private resource, but also as a social institution on which the edifice of the market economy is built.

Concerning defences to tort claims for interference with property rights, little has been said chiefly because there are few relevant defences to the typical tort claim in this area. Contributory negligence may, of course, provide a defence to a claim for negligent damage to property, as may assumption of risk and illegality. Apart from consent, the only possible defence to a claim for possession would be that the dispossessor had a better right to possession than the person in actual possession. Legal authority may provide an answer to a claim for taking possession of property, for entry to property and for nuisance, but is unlikely to be available in other types of case. As we have seen, mistake as to the existence of the harm-sufferer's property right is rarely an answer; nor can the harm-doer normally plead that the interference was neither intended nor negligent.

Consent is a pivotal idea throughout this area of the law. In many cases, lack of consent to the interference is an element of the claim: for instance, trespass is defined as an act unconsented to by the landowner. An important exception is nuisance, where not only is lack of consent not an element of the claim, but also it is no defence for the harm-doer to say that the nuisance existed before the harm-sufferer came into proximity with it.

3. CONTRACTUAL INTERESTS

As we saw in Chapter 4, tort law protects contractual interests from interference by the other party to a contract and by 'third parties'.

THIRD-PARTY INTERFERENCE WITH CONTRACTUAL RIGHTS

There are, essentially, two types of third-party interference with contractual rights that tort law classifies as wrongful: inducing a party to a contract not to perform it and disabling a party to a contract from performing it. The basic difference between these two types of interference is that the former operates through the mind of the contracting party whereas the latter does not. Actionable inducement may take the form of persuasion (by pointing out advantages to the contracting party in non-performance or disadvantages in performance) or threatening the contracting party with adverse consequences if they perform (intimidation). Damage is the gist of interference with contract. Persuasion and threats are, by their very nature, deliberate acts, whereas disablement may not, per se, be deliberate. However, there can be no liability for interference with contractual rights unless the interferer knew (or, perhaps, ought to have known) of the existence of the relevant contractual provisions. Liability is limited by the requirement of intention: the harm-sufferer must prove that the harm-doer intended to injure.

In practice, liability for inducing breach of contract is most important in two contexts: between market competitors, and between employers and employees. In the former context, liability for inducement is supported by the desirability of preserving the security of transactions. Without stability of contracts, markets could not operate properly; and stability of contracts can be undermined just as much by inducement of breach as by breach itself. If the law allowed as justification the mere fact that the harm-doer would benefit in competition with the harm-sufferer by persuading a contracting party to breach a contract with the harm-sufferer, the whole market system would be undermined. In fact, the only sort of justification recognised by law for inducement of breach of contract by persuasion is that the harm-doer did it to protect their own legal rights or, possibly, some public interest, which the law considers to be 'superior' to the contractual right of the innocent contracting party.

Between employers and employees, inducing breach of contract is, in legal terms, the prime method by which unions organise strikes and other forms of industrial action, and liability for such inducement is the main basis on which employers can legally attack strikes. The law in this area has, for the past century, been a complex amalgam of common law

and statute, the former laying down the basic rule of liability for inducing breach of contract, and the latter defining an area of 'immunity'
from liability the size of which has varied from time to time according to
changing political and social views about the desirable balance between
the interests of 'capital' on the one hand and of 'labour' on the other. In
this context more than any other, tort law has been at the forefront of
bitter arguments about the (ab)use and control of economic power in
society. Here, the link between the rights and obligations created by tort
law to regulate interactions between individuals, and large economic and
political questions about the sort of society we want to live in, could not
be clearer. (For more on this see Chapter 8).

In tort law, inducing someone not to perform a contract by threatening them is called 'intimidation'. Intimidation (as opposed to inducement
by 'persuasion') is tortious only if what the harm-doer threatened to do
would be unlawful (criminal, for instance). Threatening to do something
lawful cannot be tortious. Similarly, it can be tortious to disable a person from performing their contract with another only if the disabling
conduct was itself unlawful. The justification for the requirement of
unlawfulness is, perhaps, that much perfectly legitimate market activity involves intentionally inflicting harm on another. The requirement
of unlawfulness may be seen as an additional protection for competitive activity. On the other hand, it is one thing to intend to force your
competitors out of business, but another to do so by inducing or causing
others to breach their contracts with your competitors.

TORT LIABILITY OF CONTRACTING PARTIES

Some breaches of contract are also actionable ('concurrently') as torts by
the innocent party to the contract. This is because one and the same set
of facts may contain the elements of more than one cause of action and
may amount to more than one legal wrong (see more on this in Chapter 6).
Not all breaches of contract are actionable as torts. The paradigm of a
breach of contract actionable as a tort is negligent misfeasance causing physical or financial loss. Contractual nonfeasance is less likely to
be actionable in tort because (as we have seen) nonfeasance is, in general, less likely than misfeasance to be actionable in tort. Non-negligent
breach of contract is also less likely to be tortious because there are few
relevant grounds of strict tort liability.

CONTRACTUAL OPPORTUNITIES

Contracts are an important legal vehicle for the mutually advantageous transfer of goods and services from one person to another, and they are the basic legal form of market activity. A corollary of the importance of contract to the operation of a market economy is the basic principle of 'freedom of contract': people should be free to make what contracts they choose with whom they choose, or not to contract at all. For the protection of weaker parties, this principle is much modified by statutory provisions and, to a lesser extent, by common-law rules of contract law. However, it is still the law's starting point. The part tort law plays in protecting contractual freedom is to provide remedies for two types of interference with its exercise. The first is preventing someone exercising their freedom to contract or, in other words, to deprive someone of opportunities to contract. This is sometimes called 'interference with trade'. The second, conversely, is inducing someone to exercise their freedom to contract or in other words, to take an opportunity to contract.

Deprivation

The essence of competition is interference with the contractual expectancies of others by luring away their customers. Extensive tort liability for depriving others of contractual opportunities could undermine competition to an unacceptable extent. Tort law reflects ideas about the sorts of competitive activities that are fair or, by contrast, unfair. The other main practical area of operation of tort rules about deprivation of contracting opportunities is that of trade disputes between employees and employers. Besides inducing breach of contract, deprivation of contractual opportunities is a typical form of industrial action.

Three torts are mainly relevant here: conspiracy, intimidation and causing loss by unlawful means (or, as I will call it, 'unlawful interference with trade'). Three devices are used to limit the scope of these torts. First, interference can be tortious only if the harm-doer intended to cause damage to the harm-sufferer by depriving them of contractual opportunities. Negligent interference with opportunities to contract is generally not tortious. This rule is designed to preserve competition which, by its very nature, often involves such conduct. In non-competitive contexts, the rule is probably based on the idea that people should take steps to protect themselves from negligent, non-competitive interference with their trading interests.

Second, it is generally not tortious to deprive another of contractual opportunities by conduct (or 'means') not intrinsically unlawful (not criminal, for instance). The only exception is the form of conspiracy called 'simple conspiracy'. A conspiracy is, essentially, an agreement. There are two forms of tortious conspiracy: 'simple conspiracy', which does not involve the use of unlawful means, and 'unlawful means conspiracy' which (obviously) does. The traditional view of conspiracy is that the element of agreement or combination is important in justifying the imposition of liability. This explains why an agreement to do a lawful act with the intention of injuring another's trade may be tortious even when such conduct by one person acting alone would not be. Liability for simple conspiracy is now widely thought to be unfair. The requirement of unlawfulness is considered crucially important in preventing the legal concept of 'unfair competition' getting too far out of step with ideas of commercial morality, and unduly restricting competition.

A third device used to limit the scope of these torts is the defence of justification. The defence is most important in relation to simple conspiracy—in this context, commercial self-interest justifies agreements to injure another. Where the means used were unlawful, commercial self-interest would be unlikely to provide a defence. Indeed, in general, the use of unlawful means would typically be difficult to justify.

Besides common-law torts, there are various important statutory grounds of liability for deprivation of opportunities to contract. For example, one of the main aims of the Sex Discrimination Act 1975 and the Race Relations Act 1976 is to protect against deprivation of employment or other contracting opportunities on grounds of sex or race. In contrast to the position under the common law, liability is strict; but the conduct proscribed by these statutes is narrowly defined. There are various other statutory causes of action, directed at anti-competitive practices in various sectors of the economy, involving refusals to contract with certain individuals or refusals to contract except on onerous terms. However, the common law and statutory torts play only a very minor part in protecting market participants from unfair practices. Because of the large-scale nature of much anti-competitive activity, government regulation and the criminal law are thought to be more effective than individual tort actions in controlling such activity. For the same reason, individual tort actions

in this area would often pose large economic questions about the operation of the market that courts think better and more properly dealt with
by non-judicial governmental bodies.

Inducement of Contracting

The essence of this species of wrong is inducing a person to enter a contract by making a false statement about how financially beneficial the
contract is likely to be. The contract may, but need not, be with the maker
of the statement. There are two relevant common-law torts: deceit and
negligent misstatement. There is no strict common-law tort liability for
false statements except for defamatory statements. Deceit (or 'fraud')
involves making a false statement knowing it to be false, or not caring
whether it is true or false, with the intention of inducing a person to rely
on it to their detriment.

Liability for negligent misstatement arises only if the harm-doer
'assumed responsibility' to the harm-sufferer for the truth of the statement (*Hedley Byrne v Heller* [1964] AC 465). This opaque concept is
designed to mark out those cases in which it is reasonable to allow a person to rely on the accuracy of another's statement without taking independent advice. In cases where the maker of the statement is the other
party to the contract, the law will treat the former as having assumed
responsibility. In other cases, there is no general principle that determines when someone will be treated as having assumed responsibility
for their statements. However, it has been held, for instance, that an auditor who makes negligent misstatements about the financial position of a
company is not liable in tort to purchasers of shares in the company who
rely on the auditor's report (*Caparo Plc v Dickman* [1990] 2 AC 605).

The concept of assumption of responsibility suggests a distinction
between obligations imposed on a person and obligations voluntarily
undertaken by that person. There is a strong underlying assumption in
much discussion of tort law that whereas it is acceptable to impose on
people, regardless of their will, obligations to avoid causing physical injuries to persons and property, the law should recognise an obligation to
avoid causing financial harm only where a person has, in some sense,
taken it upon themselves by deliberate conduct (such as by making a
contract). This is because, in general, we expect people to do more to
protect their own financial interests than their physical interests.
However, the words 'in general' are of great significance. Tort law imposes

various obligations designed to protect financial interests in property. For instance, unauthorised exploitation of property can be tortious not because of any obligation undertaken by the exploiter but because, on the contrary, the exploiter did not contract with the owner for the use of the property. What's more, because assumption of responsibility is judged objectively, the concept normally signals imposition of a new obligation rather than reinforcement of a voluntarily-accepted obligation.

In addition to the common-law heads of tort liability, there are various statutory heads of tort liability for negligent misstatement under statutes such as the Misrepresentation Act 1967 (section 2(1)) and the Financial Services Act 1986.

4. NON-CONTRACTUAL OPPORTUNITIES

A non-contractual opportunity is a chance to secure financial gains by means other than the making of an advantageous contract. For example (as we noted in Chapter 4), until the testator dies, a named beneficiary under a will has a non-contractual opportunity to receive a legacy. If, because of negligence on the part of a lawyer, the intended beneficiary fails to receive the legacy, the lawyer may be liable for the value of the expected gift. The technical explanation of the liability is that the lawyer assumes responsibility to the beneficiary (even if the lawyer has no contact with the beneficiary and even if, at the time of the alleged negligence, the beneficiary knew nothing either of the testator, the will or the lawyer). Underlying this technicality is the idea that once the testator has died, nothing can be done to perfect the beneficiary's intended claim on the testator's estate; and since the beneficiary could not reasonably have been expected to do anything to protect his or her own financial interest, the negligent lawyer should pay.

In practice, the most important source of protection for non-contractual opportunities in tort law is the Fatal Accidents Act 1976. Where a person's death was the result of a tort, a 'fatal accident' claim may be brought under the Act on behalf of any of a specified list of 'dependants' of the deceased. The prime purpose of such a claim is to compensate intimates of the deceased for loss of (actual and) expected financial support. In general, tort law does not compensate a person for 'relational' financial harm flowing from injuries to another (as opposed to the other's death) or from damage to property owned by another. Suppose, for instance, that a vessel negligently collides with a public bridge over a river that divides two parts of a city, putting it out of action and causing financial loss to people who regularly use it. Tort law does not protect the users from such financial harm

Tort law's unwillingness to compensate for relational financial harm is often said to arise from a fear of floods of actions by people with a more-or-less remote financial stake in the other's activities, and a desire not to impose 'unfair burdens' on potential harm-doers. In modern society, we might say, the autonomy and separate identity of individuals is highly-prized. If I injure someone, my responsibility is to that person above all, and to those members of the person's immediate family who are most closely affected. The web of financial interdependencies in society is large and complex, but once we get beyond the centre of the web, people are expected to take steps to protect their own financial interests. The list of classes of claimants in the Fatal Accidents Act (based on some idea of family intimacy) represents the law's attempt to describe what is meant by 'the centre of the web'.

5. TRADE VALUES

The term 'trade values' refers to the interest in exploiting the fruits of one's skill and effort for financial gain. One way in which the law protects trade values is by creating property rights in them ('intellectual property') and making interference with such rights tortious. Most intellectual property rights and their associated protective torts are statutory. A person may also be able to protect their trade values by contract—franchising and 'character merchandising' are common examples. For the 'creator', one of the main advantages of the property technique over the contractual is that property rights can be enforced against people generally, whereas contractual rights can only be enforced against those who have made contracts for the exploitation of the trade value.

It is often suggested that the common law should recognise a general principle of liability for unauthorised exploitation of trade values—or, in a long-established pithy phrase, for 'reaping without sowing'. English courts have always resisted the adoption of so general a principle of liability for 'unfair competition', essentially on the ground that it is best left to the legislature to decide how far and by what means the law should protect the interests of creators in exploiting their creative powers for financial gain. The only important judicial activity in this area is found in the law of passing-off. The essence of passing-off, as developed in the nineteenth century, was causing loss to another by misrepresenting your own goods or services to be those of another person, thus confusing consumers into buying your own goods or services instead of the other person's. Courts have frequently been asked to extend passing-off to cases involving neither misrepresentation nor confusion, and they have made some moves in this direction in recent years. However, the tort of passing-off is still a long way from embodying the principle against reaping without sowing.

6. FINANCIAL HARM

Finally, we must examine cases in which the form of the complaint is simply that as a result of the harm-doer's conduct, the harm-sufferer is financially worse-off. Some grounds of tort liability for intentional conduct, such as malicious prosecution, abuse of legal process and liability for misfeasance in public office, may provide a basis for such a complaint. A claim that as a result of a misstatement by the harm-doer (whether fraudulent or negligent) the harm-sufferer gave money away to a third party, would fall into this category.

As we saw earlier, tort law is reluctant to compensate for 'relational' financial harm. In some cases of relational harm there may be a contract between the harm-sufferer and the injured party. For instance, a person may suffer financial harm as a result of damage to a piece of property that the harm-sufferer rents from the injured party. A person may suffer non-contractual relational harm where, for instance, a citizen suffers financially as a result of closure of a public bridge after it is damaged by negligent navigation of a vessel by the harm-doer. In general, people are expected to protect themselves from relational harm. In the contractual case, such protection might take the form of a provision in the contract. In the non-contractual case, it might take the form of insurance.

A person may suffer financial harm as a result of paying too much (ie more than their value) for substandard services, or shoddy goods or premises. The general rule of common law is that such loss is recoverable in a tort action for negligence only if the harm-doer (the provider of the services or the vendor of the goods) 'assumed responsibility' for the quality of the services or goods. We have already observed the opaqueness of this criterion of liability, and it is necessary to say a little more about when a defendant might be treated as having assumed responsibility.

In the first place, it seems that the negligent provider of a financial service is more likely to be held to have assumed responsibility than the negligent builder of premises or producer of goods. Indeed, there is much authority for the proposition that under normal circumstances, builders and manufacturers do not assume responsibility to purchasers of their output for the quality of that output, and so are not normally liable to them in tort for purely financial loss flowing from the defectiveness of the output. Second, whether an assumption of responsibility will be found depends partly on a judgment of the court about whether it would be reasonable to expect the harm-sufferer to protect his or her own financial interests. In one case, for example, it was held that a ship surveyor, who negligently certified for the owner that a ship was seaworthy, was not liable in tort, to the owner of cargo being carried on the ship, for financial loss suffered when the ship sank and the cargo was lost (*Marc Rich & Co AG v Bishop Rock Marine Co Ltd (The Nicholas H)* [1996] AC 211). The underlying rationale of the decision appears to be that it was reasonable to expect the cargo owner, which was a commercial entity, to protect itself from such financial loss by taking out insurance.

The decision was also probably influenced by the fact that the surveyor was not the immediate cause of the loss of the cargo. The immediate cause was that an unseaworthy ship went to sea. The surveyor's negligent act merely failed to prevent the loss of the cargo. It might be said that the person primarily responsible for maintaining the ship in a seaworthy condition and for the decision to put to sea was the ship owner; and that the surveyor was only secondarily responsible for the condition of the ship and the decision to sail. Courts are less willing to hold that a party, secondarily responsible in this causal sense, has 'assumed responsibility' for economic loss than to hold that a primarily responsible party has. Courts are also extremely reluctant to impose tort liability on a harm-doer for failure to protect another from purely financial loss unless the harm-doer has been paid to provide protection. Even if there is a contract between the harm-sufferer and the harm-doer, liability for failure to protect a person from financial loss may only be imposed if the contract expressly requires the harm-doer to provide protection. Put another way, the most the law will normally do is to reinforce an undertaking to provide protection based on deliberate conduct of the harm-doer creating the undertaking.

6

Wrongs

KI 4: Torts are only one species of legal wrongs

It will be clear from the last two chapters—in which the catalogue of torts has been unpacked and repackaged in terms of protected interests and harmful conduct—that torts are only one type of legal wrong. Other types include crimes, breaches of contract, and so on. This raises two questions that this chapter aims to answer. First, what is the relationship between torts and other legal wrongs? And second, is there anything distinctive about torts as a species of legal wrong?

1. THE PLACE OF TORT LAW IN THE LEGAL UNIVERSE

PRIVATE LAW AND PUBLIC LAW

Lawyers divide the law into various categories. One of the major divisions is between private law and public law. Private law is concerned basically with relations between 'private' individuals (including corporations). Public law is concerned with relations between private individuals ('the governed'), and government (or 'the governors'), as well as between government entities. Constitutional law and administrative law are two categories within public law.

Tort law is part of private law. It was developed primarily to regulate social interactions between ordinary individuals. However, it also applies to interactions between government and the governed, and even between government entities. This reflects the original concept of government in

England according to which government is not a distinct legal entity in its own right but merely a collection of individuals ('citizens in uniform': Gardner 2012b) with distinctive powers and functions. The original governors were the Monarch and Crown officials. Today, the governors are, effectively, the Prime Minister and Ministers of State. Of course, in modern times, the distinction between government officials and ordinary citizens is clearly marked and governments are understood to have 'public' functions. The differences between governors and governed make application of 'private' tort law to relations between citizens and government one of the most difficult and complex topics in tort law. Despite its importance, considerations of space prevent further discussion in this book.

THE LAW OF INTERESTS AND THE LAW OF OBLIGATIONS

Another basic division within private law is between the 'law of interests' (my term) and the 'law of obligations' (a term in common use). By 'the law of interests' I mean law that creates the various types of interests discussed in Chapter 4 and other legally protected interests. The law of obligations is concerned with the protection of legal interests. Tort law is largely a law of obligations. It does not typically create the interests it protects. For instance, property interests are created by property law, which is mainly a law of interests. Contractual interests are created by contract law, which is also concerned with protection of the interests it creates. Interests in personal health and safety are usually thought of as existing independently of law (as 'human rights' if you like), which recognises rather than creates them.

The law of obligations is normally divided into the categories of tort law, contract law, the law of restitution (or 'unjust enrichment') and the law of equity (including the law of trusts). These categories provide a convenient way of grouping together causes of action that are related to each other in some way. Like tort law, each of these categories could be unpacked and repackaged in terms of protected interests and harmful conduct. That is a task for others. Our interest in categories of the law of obligations is to find out what we can learn about tort law and its distinctiveness by looking at its relationship to these other categories.

TORT LAW AND CONTRACT LAW

The law of contract protects financial interests in the form of contractual rights and contractual opportunities. It also protects against bodily injury and death, mental injury and, in certain circumstances, anxiety and inconvenience; and it protects against physical damage to tangible property. The standards of liability recognised in contract law are negligence and strict liability. Contract law does not recognise intentional conduct as an independent form of wrongdoing—in other words, it creates no obligations that can only be breached intentionally.

With very few exceptions, contract law provides protection only to the parties to a contract, and not to third parties affected by the contract. In other words, contract law mainly protects parties who are already in a contractual relationship with one another. We have seen that tort law also sometimes protects the interests of parties who are in a contractual relationship with one another: breach of contract can sometimes also amount to a tort against the other party to the contract. In tort law, the fact that the harm-doer and the harm-sufferer are in some sort of relevant non-contractual relationship such as parent and child, or prisoner and gaoler, or occupier of land and visitor, does not, of course, disentitle the harm-sufferer from tort law's protection. For instance, a child may sue a parent who negligently causes bodily injury to the child. A prisoner may sue a gaoler, and a visitor may sue an occupier, in tort, for negligently inflicting personal injury, for instance. Indeed, tort law will sometimes protect interests (particularly financial interests) only if the harm-sufferer and the harm-doer were in a relevant relationship at the time of the alleged tort. The concept of 'assumption of responsibility' was invented precisely to justify imposition of tort liability by establishing a relationship between the harm-doer and the harm-sufferer created in advance of the alleged tort.

However, one of the most distinctive features of the obligations that tort law imposes, as compared with those typically imposed by contract law, is that the harm-doer and the harm-sufferer need normally have been in no relevant relationship at the time of the alleged tort. The most common type of tort claim is one arising out of a road accident. In the typical road accident, the harm-sufferer is a 'stranger' to the harm-doer; but this lack of relationship is no bar to a claim in tort by the harm-sufferer.

For a long time, harm-sufferers have attempted to exploit this difference between tort obligations and contractual obligations to overcome the lack of a pre-existing relationship with a harm-doer. *Donoghue v Stevenson* [1932] AC 562 established that the consumer of a defective product could sue the manufacturer in tort for personal injury caused by use of the product even though the consumer was completely unknown to the manufacturer, had no contractual relationship with the manufacturer and, indeed, had a contractual relationship with the café owner who sold the consumer the allegedly defective ginger beer. The court was not prepared to deny the harm-sufferer a tort claim against the manufacturer on the basis that she had a contractual relationship with the café owner and could have sued him in contract. By contrast, tort law is very reluctant to protect financial interests in this way. Typically in such cases, if a harm-sufferer has a relevant contractual relationship with a party other than the harm-doer, tort law will not protect their interest against interference by the harm-doer.

Another distinctive difference between the way contract law and tort law respectively protect interests is that contract law, unlike tort law, commonly imposes strict liability for nonfeasance. Another way of putting this is to say that failure to bring about a specified state of affairs may be a breach of contract even though the failure was not the result of faulty conduct; but cannot be a tort. In the law of contract a person may be liable simply because a state of affairs does not materialise, full stop. Furthermore, the law of tort is more-or-less reluctant to impose liability for negligent nonfeasance or, in other words, negligent failure to prevent injury or loss occurring (as opposed to causing injury or loss). By contrast, a contract is a means by which a legally enforceable obligation to take care to protect another from injury or loss may be created. A main distinguishing feature of the law of contract, compared with the law of tort, is a greater willingness to impose strict and negligence-based liability for nonfeasance. In other words, contract provides a technique for creating legally enforceable obligations of positive action, both strict obligations and obligations to take care.

One way of explaining the relationship between tort law and contract law is to say that tort law provides a basic measure of legal protection for a wide range of interests. If a party seeks legal protection for an interest that tort law does not protect, or protection for an interest that tort law does protect, greater than that provided by tort law, contract may provide a technique for securing such protection. Put slightly differently, it may be possible to 'buy' protection greater than tort law provides by entering a contract. The possibility, by contract, of creating strict obligations of positive action is what makes it the prime legal mechanism for wealth creation and the productive exchange of resources.

TORT LAW AND THE LAW OF EQUITY

Historically there was a deep chasm between the common law (developed by the common-law courts), of which the law of tort was a part, and the law of trusts and equitable obligations (developed by the courts of Chancery, or 'Equity'). As we noted previously, the distinction between 'common law' and 'equity' was a function of the fact that there were two separate sets of courts. Chancery started out as a mechanism through which citizens could petition the Monarch (through the Lord Chancellor) to reverse decisions of the Monarch's judges that they considered unjust— hence, the law that Chancery applied came to be called 'equity'. Although the institutional division between common-law courts and equity courts was effectively abolished in the nineteenth century, the distinction between rules and principles of 'law', developed by the common-law courts, and rules and principles of 'equity' (developed by the Chancery Court) lingers on and has significant effects on tort law, which was developed by the common-law courts. Amongst the concepts developed 'in Chancery' that the common-law courts did not make use of, three stand out as particularly important for understanding tort law. They are 'equitable property', 'fiduciary obligation' and 'unconscionability'.

Equitable Property Interests

The term 'equitable property' describes the interest of the beneficiary under a trust. The trust is a technique by which obligations can be imposed on the owner of (tangible or intangible) property (the 'trustee') to use that property for the benefit of another ('the beneficiary'). The beneficiary's rights are enforceable not only against the trustee but also against certain third parties who acquire the trust property. The basic function of equitable property rights is different from the function of what may be called 'common-law' property interests such as are protected by the torts of trespass and conversion. The basic function of common-law property rights is to allocate assets to individuals and distribute resources in society—to determine 'what is yours and what is mine'. The basic function of equitable property rights is to control the way in which common-law property is used. A person who has common-law rights over property must exercise those rights for the benefit of the beneficiary of the trust rather than for their own benefit.

Traditionally, liability for interference with common-law property rights was conceptualised as common-law tort liability, and liability for interference with equitable property rights was conceptualised as equitable liability. In other words, whereas the law of tort was the main source of legal protection for common-law property rights (including the common-law property rights of trustees), it was not a source of protection for equitable property rights. This was a result of the jurisdictional divide between the common law and the equity courts. Nevertheless, most of the building blocks of equitable liability for breach of trust by trustees, and for interference with the beneficiary's interests by third parties, are present in tort law. Depending on the nature of the breach, a trustee's liability is either strict or negligence-based; and when it is negligence-based, the standard of reasonable conduct is in some circumstances 'ordinary negligence' and in others 'extraordinary negligence' (see page 43 above). The liability of third parties is similarly based on the concepts of deliberate, intentional and reckless conduct which, as we have seen, are also used in tort law. The distinctiveness of the equitable wrongs of breach of trust and interference with trust rests in the types of interest protected, namely the interest of one person in the use of property belonging to another. However, it is 'historical accident' that this type of interest in property is not protected by tort law while others are. Breach of trust and interference with trust are, effectively, (equitable) torts.

Fiduciary Obligations

The essential idea underlying the trust is that one person (the trustee) must use property for the benefit of another and not for their own benefit. This same idea underlies the second of the distinctive features of equity law, namely fiduciary obligations. Trustees are fiduciaries, but not all fiduciaries are trustees. A person may be under an obligation to act for the benefit of another (the 'principal') even if 'the fiduciary' owns no property in which the principal has an interest. For instance, a solicitor is in a fiduciary relationship with the client. In the capacity of solicitor, the solicitor must act for the benefit of the client and not for his or her own benefit. If a fiduciary makes a gain by improperly exploiting their fiduciary position, the fiduciary must surrender that gain to the person for whose benefit the fiduciary ought to have acted. The fiduciary's obligation is strict and is designed to prevent the exploitation of conflicts of interest, even if innocent. It sits alongside the contractual and tortious obligations of the lawyer to the client.

Fiduciary obligations are different from any obligation imposed by tort law. Generally, tort law does not require people to act for the benefit of others and to ignore their own interests, but only to avoid causing harm to others. The only basis on which tort law imposes strict liability for gains is exploitation of another's property without consent. The liability of a trustee to a beneficiary for exploiting trust property for the trustee's own benefit is like this type of tort liability. However, the idea of fiduciary obligation can be used to impose property-independent obligations to act for the benefit of another. Strict, property-independent obligations to act for the benefit of another are a distinctive product of equity. Nevertheless, it is, once again, merely a 'product of history' that such obligations were invented 'in Chancery' and not 'at common law'.

Unconscionable Conduct

The Chancery Court, it is commonly said, was a 'court of conscience'. This did not mean that equitable liability was always based on 'unconscionable conduct'. Indeed, as we have seen, the equitable liability of trustees and fiduciaries may be strict (or negligence-based). What it did mean was that Chancery courts were sometimes prepared to give remedies for types of 'shady' conduct that the common-law courts did not recognise as wrong. For instance, whereas tort law recognises as 'fraudulent' the act of knowingly making a false statement with the intention that another should rely on it, equity would recognise as 'fraudulent' any conduct that could, in a much broader sense, be called 'unconscionable'. 'Unconscionability', like 'negligence', is a standard of conduct rather than a frame of mind. Negligence is failure to take reasonable care not to harm others by pursuing one's own interests. Unconscionability involves promoting one's own interests at the unreasonable expense of another. In general, tort law goes no further than requiring people not to harm others for the sake of their own interests, whereas equity will require people not to advance their own interests at the expense of others or, in other words, not to take unfair advantage of others.

In English law, these two different ethical standards—do not harm others and do not take advantage of others—are identified with two different bodies of law: common law and equity respectively. Integrating these two, historically-distinct bodies of law would involve working out an acceptable relationship between legitimate self-seekingness (limited by a duty not to harm) and the proper demands of altruism (expressed in the idea that one should not take unfair advantage of others).

TORT LAW AND THE LAW OF RESTITUTION

The law of restitution (or 'unjust enrichment') is concerned with gains wrongfully received as opposed to harm wrongfully inflicted. To a limited extent, tort law is concerned about unjust enrichment. Most importantly (as already noted), tort law sometimes recognises gains made by exploiting another's property as wrongful regardless of whether any harm was inflicted on the property-owner in the process. For instance, a person who 'converts' another's chattel by using it for their own purposes and to their own benefit may be required to 'disgorge' the gains made by using the property even if the property was in no way harmed by the use, even if the owner would not have made use of the property if the gain-maker had not, and even if the user honestly and reasonably believed the property to be their own. This is strict tort liability for making gains out of another's property.

The law of restitution goes even further than this. In certain circumstances, it will require one person to return (or 'restore') to another person something handed over by the other in the mistaken belief that they had an obligation to hand it over, even if the recipient did nothing to induce the mistaken belief and took no part in the transfer. Suppose, for instance, that unbeknownst to D, C mistakenly makes an electronic transfer of funds to D's bank account. In this type of case, the trigger of the obligation to restore is not receipt of the payment by D: D was not in any sense responsible for the making of the payment and could not have done anything to prevent the payment being made. If D is to be required to restore the payment it can only be on the basis that once D knows that the payment was made by mistake, it would be unfair of D to retain it, unless D has 'changed position' since receiving the payment (but before learning of the mistake) in such a way as to make it unfair to require restoration. In such a case, the law steps in, despite the fact that D has done nothing wrong and, maybe, has done nothing relevant at all. D has done no harm to C and made no gain by exploiting C or C's property.

Here, then, we have a legal obligation and liability that would seem truly out of place in a tort law book. If there is one thing that all torts have in common it is that they are 'wrongs'. Of course, this does not distinguish torts from other legal wrongs such as breaches of contract and breaches of trust—which leaves us with the question of whether there is anything distinctive about tort law?

2. THE DISTINCTIVENESS OF TORT LAW

In fact, the distinctiveness, such as it is, of tort law within the category of private law seems to lie mostly in the interests which it protects. The law of torts is the predominant source of legal protection for interests in the person. Tort law is also the main source of legal protection for common-law (as opposed to equitable) property interests, for contractual opportunities and for reputation. It is true, of course, that these interests can also be protected by contract law; but tort law protects them in their own right and for their own sake, not because of an agreement to protect them. Perhaps the most characteristic feature of tort law is its concern to protect people against wrongdoing by 'strangers' with whom they have no relevant relationship at the time of the wrong. Tort law sometimes requires such a relationship, but only exceptionally. Ironically, the word that Lord Atkin used (in *Donoghue v Stevenson* [1932] AC 562) to convey tort law's concern with strangers was 'neighbour'; but he used this word to refer to all those around us who are potentially affected by our wrongful conduct: my neighbour is anyone whom I should avoid wronging, even complete strangers. This characteristic feature helps to explain tort law's apparent lack of unity: there are many ways in which we can wrong our neighbours, and this is reflected in the diversity and variety of tort law and torts.

This characteristic of tort law helps us to understand why it began to outgrow the confines of the formulary system many years before that system was abolished. The birth of the modern law of torts can be traced to the late eighteenth century and the beginnings of the Industrial Revolution. One result of industrialisation was to increase the size of communities and contact groups. This happened as a result of urbanisation and the invention of new means of transport and communication that enabled people, goods and information to travel further and faster than ever before. Urbanisation increased social anonymity and brought people together into much larger and more complex 'neighbourhoods' (in Lord Atkin's sense). At the same time, faster means of transport and myriad new forms of powered machinery greatly increased the physical and other risks associated with living in these larger neighbourhoods. These processes alert us to two basic features of law: it is both a social and an evolutionary phenomenon. There is a two-way interaction between law and social life, each affecting the other in complex ways. Law evolves by adapting to social change at the same time as preserving sufficient continuity to hold societies together through times of rapid change. Parts of what we now think of as tort law existed long before the Industrial Revolution, but it is the character of being a law for 'neighbourhoods of strangers' that makes modern tort law distinctive.

And things go on changing. For instance, during the course of the twentieth century, tort law reflected and adapted to the invention of the internal combustion engine and the motor car just as in the nineteenth it adapted to the advent of steam railways and the ecology of the factory. In the West, the late twentieth century witnessed the beginnings of the Information Revolution; and tort law has reflected this change. As much industrial production has moved to the Global South, tort law has come to play a much lesser role than previously in protecting the physical interests of industrial workers, while dramatic increases in travel and mobility have brought its role in dealing with traffic accidents even more to the fore. And just as (statutory) tort law adapted, for instance, to the invention of the printing press by creating intellectual property rights such as copyright, so at the beginning of the twenty-first century tort law will have to adapt to the digital economy.

Much scholarly work has been done on the history of tort law and the symbiotic interaction between legal doctrine and social change, especially during the nineteenth century; but the social history of English tort law remains largely unwritten. The story will necessarily be complex if it is to make sense of the law in the books in the light of changing social needs, political structures, judicial practice and moral values, and their mutual interactions. It is certainly no exaggeration to say that by understanding tort law 'in the round' as a social and historical phenomenon we understand something of what it means to be human. This is one very good reason for studying tort law in all its richness and diversity.

7

Out and About with Tort Law

KI 5: Tort law is rarely enforced

1. CONFORMITY, IMPLEMENTATION AND ENFORCEMENT

To see the truth contained in this key idea it will help to draw two distinctions: between conforming to and complying with tort law (doctrine); and between implementing and enforcing tort law (doctrine).

CONFORMITY AND COMPLIANCE

From the pages of statutes, law reports and textbooks, tort law addresses its intended audience(s) in a monologue. Otherwise, it is inert. Like law generally, tort law addresses at least two distinct audiences: it speaks to all of us as its subjects, and it speaks to the group of officials and institutions involved in delivering the remedies that tort law provides for wrongful interference with protected interests.

Let's think about tort law's subjects first. Tort law speaks from the pages of the law books. Most of tort law's subjects never read the law books. Some—especially commercial entities—are advised about what the books say by lawyers who do read them. Newspaper publishers, for instance, may have in-house lawyers to consult about the tort law of defamation. But most people know little about tort law. They would probably be amazed to learn how much tort law there actually is, and how relevant it is to their everyday lives. At the same time, however, many people would not be so surprised when they heard about what tort law says. They would probably consider most of the obligations it imposes quite reasonable—'common-sense morality', even. There is a feedback loop between tort law and prevalent views in society about right and wrong. Many legal norms are imported into the law from other social normative systems, and when law adds to or departs from prevalent social views it tends to seep into, and supplement or modify, those other social normative systems. Most people, most of the time, are inclined to do what the tort law requires not because (they know that) the law requires it but because their own value systems require it. This, we might think, is the only basis on which it is fair to say that 'ignorance of the law is no excuse' (Goodin 2010).

Of course, torts are not rare events. For instance, each year in England there are about one million successful, recorded personal-injury tort claims mostly arising out of road accidents. Intentional physical violence is one of the most common forms of recorded criminality; and much intentional physical violence is also tortious. Given tort law's stringent understanding of defamation, there is no doubt a lot of it about. Still, it is probably also a fair guess that most people, most of the time, aim to drive carefully; and even when they are negligent in the tortious sense, their carelessness rarely causes accidents. Most people rarely, if ever, intentionally do physical violence to others or knowingly commit actionable defamation. Let's say that when people behave in the way that tort law requires, they conform to tort law; and let's speculate that most people conform to tort law most of the time. Conformity is all the law requires. It does not demand compliance in the sense of doing what the law requires because the law requires it. It is satisfied with conformity.

IMPLEMENTATION AND ENFORCEMENT

Now let's turn to the other audience addressed by tort law: officials and institutions involved in providing remedies for torts when subjects fail to conform. When we think of remedying torts we tend to conjure up courts in our mind. However, courts are very rarely directly involved in remedying torts. For instance, less than one per cent of the one million or so tort claims per year ever get anywhere near a court. There is a court hearing in only a very small number of cases, and in most, court proceedings are not even commenced. What is distinctive about the way courts process tort claims is that they can make orders (to pay money, for instance) that are ultimately enforceable by the power of the state—by 'sending in the sheriff', for instance. Courts, in short, can 'enforce' tort law by making 'remedial orders' enforceable by legal officials.

Tort law rarely needs to be enforced in this way. Remedies are available only against people who fail to conform to tort law's demands. But it turns out that most non-conformers do not have to be forced by the power of the state to remedy their torts. Instead, the typical non-conformer against whom a tort claim is made agrees with the harm-sufferer to remedy the tort, and complies with the agreement. The process of making such agreements between tort claimants and tort defendants is usually referred to as 'settlement out of court'. Most tort claims are settled out of court by the making of a legal contract between the parties. Cases that end up in court are those in which the parties, for one reason or another, cannot agree on settlement terms. Typically, settlement contracts do not need to be, and are not, scrutinised or approved by a court.

Part of the explanation for this initially surprising state of affairs is that ultimately, legal contracts are enforceable by the power of the state. For instance, a person who fails to pay money owed under a contract can be ordered to pay the money by a court, and that order will be enforceable. In fact, however, settlement contracts in tort cases rarely need to be enforced in this way. Instead, we may say, when tort cases are settled out of court, tort law is typically implemented rather than enforced; and the main institutions of implementation are not courts but insurance companies. This is because of the widespread availability of liability insurance, which is central to the operation of tort law, especially in relation to tort claims for personal injury. In this and the following Chapters we will focus on personal-injury claims because in practice, they form the largest and most significant category of cases in which tort law is implemented and enforced. Remember, however, that one of the main messages of **KI 3** is that tort law protects a diverse range of interests of which the interest in personal health and safety is only one. The way tort law protects these other interests in practice also deserves (but has generally not received) analysis and investigation.

2. LIABILITY INSURANCE

As its name implies, liability insurance protects against the risk of being held liable to pay damages for a tort or other legal wrong.

Liability insurance was first used in the shipping industry and was well-developed in that context by the mid-nineteenth century. The catalyst for development of a market in insurance against the risk of liability for personal injury was provided not by developments in tort law but by the enactment, in the late-nineteenth century, of legislation imposing strict statutory obligations on employers to compensate workers injured on the job ('workmen's compensation', as it was originally called) designed to overcome defects in the common law of employers' liability (tort) law. The fledgling liability insurance industry received a significant boost from the development of the motorcar in the early-twentieth century. By the 1920s, road accidents had become such a social problem that in 1930, legislation was enacted making it compulsory for users of motor vehicles on public roads to take out liability insurance covering personal injuries caused to other road users. It is difficult to overestimate the significance of the introduction of compulsory liability insurance for the implementation and enforcement of tort doctrine.

Imagine a world in which tort doctrine applied to road accidents but liability insurance was not available. As potential harm-doers, people would face the risk of being ordered to pay compensatory damages, which they would have to do out of their own resources if they could. As potential harm-sufferers, people would face the risk of being unable to recover damages awarded to them from harm-doers who lacked the resources to pay. Both groups could face financial ruin.

Now imagine a world in which tort doctrine applied, and there was a market in liability insurance, but car-users were free not to purchase such insurance. By choosing not to purchase liability insurance, potential harm-doers who lacked sufficient resources to pay a significant award of compensatory damages (the majority?) could make themselves effectively 'judgment-proof' and not worth suing. On the other hand, potential harm-sufferers would face the risk of being injured by an uninsured driver who lacked the resources to pay. In that world, tort law would operate as a sort of lottery in which the prize was having the 'good luck' to be injured by an insured, rather than an uninsured, harm-doer.

This is the world that had come into existence in England by the late 1920s, early in the age of mass production of motor vehicles: liability insurance was readily available, but it was not compulsory for vehicle owners to buy it. The problems created by living in this world became so serious that in addition to making liability insurance compulsory, Parliament made it a criminal offence to drive without insurance and enacted various provisions designed to overcome technical problems that might make an insurance policy ineffective. It is no exaggeration to say that without compulsory road-accident liability insurance, the tort system that we have today, in which people injured in road accidents are quite reliably compensated by harm-doers, would not exist. It is also very plausible to argue that without compulsory liability insurance, tort doctrine would be different than it is in various respects. For instance, the rule that learner drivers are held to the same standard of care as experienced drivers (*Nettleship v Weston* [1971] 2 QB 691) would seem deeply unfair and highly unrealistic in a world without liability insurance. Even more importantly, the typical harm-doer could not afford to pay compensatory damages, in even a moderately serious case of personal injuries, out of their own resources and without liability insurance.

This explains why the vast majority of personal-injury tort claims are made against harm-doers who are insured against tort liability. A very small proportion are made against harm-doers who have sufficient resources to pay damages without the support of an insurer (they are sometimes call 'self-insurers'). It is a waste of time and resources to make a tort claim against a harm-doer who is not insured or who could not afford to pay damages out of their own resources. This explains why most personal-injury tort claims relate to road accidents and workplace accidents (both areas in which liability insurance is compulsory), medical-accident claims against the NHS, and 'public liability' claims against local authorities. By contrast, for instance, very few tort claims are made in relation to accidents in the home because insurance against tort liability to other occupants of the home is neither compulsory nor common.

3. IMPLEMENTATION OF TORT LAW BY INSURERS

Insurance companies settle the vast majority of cases without asking a court to determine the legal obligations of the insured defendant under tort law. For insurance companies, going to court is typically a last resort when all attempts to settle have failed. The same is more-or-less true of tort claimants, especially when they are being advised by a lawyer or an insurance company. Why are most claims against insured defendants settled? An important part of the answer is that going to court can be very expensive, and much more expensive than settling out of court. One reason for this is that to apply many of the rules of tort law accurately and properly (as a court must aim to do), it is necessary to investigate the facts of what happened, and the circumstances, causes and effects of the accident, in great detail, which can be a very costly exercise. Three issues that need to be decided in resolving tort claims deserve special mention in this respect: negligence, causation and assessment of damages.

PROOF OF NEGLIGENCE

Take the issue of negligence, first. Before it can be decided whether or not what the harm-doer did (or did not do) was negligent, it is necessary to investigate what it was that they did (or did not do), when, in what circumstances, and how. The legal concept of negligence, on which most tort claims for personal injury are based, is extremely 'fact-dependent': 'reasonableness' is judged 'in all the circumstances of the case'. Many accidents that result in personal injury occur in a very brief period of time, often in a fraction of a second. Even assuming that suitable witnesses to the accident are available, deciding the negligence issue requires them to be able to recall accurately what occurred in that fraction of a second if we are to have any confidence that what they say happened actually did happen. The unreliability of observations of eyewitnesses (even highly trained and experienced ones) is well documented. To the inaccuracies of observation must be added the difficulties of recall produced by the considerable period that often elapses between the accident and the time when witnesses are asked to give an account of what happened; and also the fact that people do not always tell the truth. If, as a result of such problems, the version of some witnesses conflicts with that of others, it may be very difficult to be confident of reaching a correct conclusion. To make matters worse, in a significant number of cases, suitable evidence is simply unavailable at all. Different, but equally difficult, problems may arise in proving fault in cases of illness or disease as opposed to traumatic accident (Stapleton 1986, chapter 4).

PROOF OF CAUSATION

Consider causation next. Of all the aspects of tort law, causation is perhaps the most complex and difficult to grasp. This is not so much (or, at least, not only) because the relevant doctrine is complex and difficult but also because the very idea of causation—of what it means to say that one thing causes another—has been a hot topic of debate amongst philosophers for thousands of years; and the disagreements and ambiguities that persist in these debates are reflected in the law. Fortunately, it is not necessary for our purposes to explore the complexities and difficulties of causation in any detail. All that is needed is to explain why investigating causation can be a very costly business.

Recall the distinction drawn earlier between 'harm' and 'damage' (see page 36–7). Damage consists of personal injury, property damage, financial loss and so on. Where the claim is that tortious conduct inflicted damage on the harm-sufferer, the harm-sufferer must prove that the tortious conduct 'caused' the damage. The legal concept of causation is an amalgam of ideas about how events are connected in the world (often called 'factual' causation) and ideas about who should take ('causal') responsibility for things that happen in the world (sometimes called 'legal' causation). Here we are concerned with factual causation, not causal responsibility. In many cases, it may be very difficult—and, hence, costly—to determine whether or not particular tortious conduct was the factual cause of particular damage.

This may be hard enough in the case of an accident that happens in a moment, for all the reasons mentioned in the earlier discussion of proof of negligence. It may be even harder in cases of medical negligence, for instance, if the question arises of whether injury suffered in the course of medical treatment was a result of (tortious) treatment or of the (non-tortious) condition being treated. Thorny problems also arise in cases where it is alleged that a person has become ill or contracted a disease as a result of being exposed to some substance or taking some drug (Stapleton 1986, chapter 3). Our knowledge of the way many diseases and illnesses come about is inadequate, and this may present an impenetrable barrier to much tort litigation. Or suppose that a person becomes ill as a result of taking medication that is made by various manufacturers, and it cannot be proved which manufacturer produced the dose that caused the illness.

Such problems, arising from 'evidentiary gaps', have been explored in recent years in a string of cases in which harm-sufferers claim to have contracted one or other of various lung diseases as a result of tortious exposure to asbestos. These cases illustrate several of the most difficult issues surrounding proof of factual causation. For instance, one of the illnesses in question is mesothelioma. All that is known about this illness is that it is caused by exposure to asbestos; but how it is caused remains a mystery. For instance, can it be caused by exposure to one fibre of asbestos or is greater exposure needed? Suppose a person is tortiously exposed to asbestos by several employers over a period of years, or that a worker is exposed to asbestos tortiously at work, but is also self-exposed in the course of DIY activities at home. Since we do not know how mesothelioma is caused, we cannot say which of the exposures caused the harm-sufferer's illness. Or suppose that a person who has smoked for many years claims to have contracted lung cancer as a result of tortious exposure to asbestos. Lung cancer has many possible causes, including smoking; but we may not know enough to be able to say, in any case in which various possible causes were operative, which (or which combination) did the harm.

How does the law deal with these and similar problems of proving factual causation? To answer this question we must first say a little more about factual causation. The basic legal test of whether tortious conduct in fact caused injury is whether the conduct was a 'necessary condition' of the injury occurring. The question is: would the injury have occurred 'but for' the tortious conduct. (Sometimes conduct will be treated as a cause even though it was not a necessary condition; but we need not explore this complication here.) In tort, the claimant must prove that the tortious conduct was a necessary condition of the harm suffered 'on the balance of probabilities'. This means that the claim will succeed only if it is 'more probable than not' that tortious conduct was the cause. In numerical terms, the harm-sufferer must prove that the conduct increased the risk of the damage by more than 100 per cent—in other words, that the conduct at least doubled the risk of the damage (say, from two in a million to five in a million). This 'balance-of-probabilities test' operates in an all-or-nothing way: if the court is satisfied that the harm-sufferer has met the test, the harm-sufferer is entitled to full compensation for the damage; but if it is not satisfied, the harm-doer escapes liability entirely. An implication of this rule about 'burden of proof' is that conduct may be held to be the cause of damage even though, in fact, the conduct was not the cause; and, conversely, that conduct may be held not to be the cause of damage even though it was the cause.

In the sorts of difficult cases of evidentiary gaps that we have been considering, the result of applying the legal test of causation using the balance-of-probabilities standard of proof may well be that the claim fails. However, this result has sometimes been thought unfair. For instance, why (it is asked) should a worker who has been tortiously exposed to asbestos by various employers over a period of years not be compensated merely because the worker cannot prove which exposure or combination of exposures caused his condition, even though we know that exposure to asbestos must have caused the mesothelioma?

Two different approaches have been tried in attempts to overcome such 'unfairness'. The first is to say that it is enough, in some cases at least, for the harm-sufferer to prove that the harm-doer's tortious conduct significantly increased the risk of the damage, even though the increase was 100 per cent or less (*Fairchild v Glenhaven Funeral Services* [2003] 1 AC 32). In cases where the increase in risk can be arithmetically quantified (say, 40 per cent), a second approach is to argue that the harm-sufferer should be able to succeed by proving, on the balance of probabilities, that because of the conduct, they lost a 40 per cent chance of avoiding the injury. The first approach involves modifying the burden of proof on the issue of factual causation, while the second involves redefining the damage that must be proved (on the balance of probabilities) to have been caused by the tortious conduct: the damage is the (40 per cent) chance of avoiding the injury, not the injury itself. Under this second approach, the compensation would be assessed as a proportion (40 per cent) of what it would be if the damage had been the injury itself. Unlike the first approach and the balance-of-probabilities test, which are all-or-nothing rules, this second approach contemplates liability 'proportional to risk'.

Both the all-or-nothing and the proportional approaches have advantages, and corresponding disadvantages for harm-sufferers and harm-doers respectively. The all-or-nothing, balance of-probabilities approach makes it relatively harder for the harm-sufferer to establish liability; but once this is done, full compensation follows. In contrast, lowering the burden of proof below balance-of-probabilities under the all-or-nothing approach disadvantages harm-doers without offering them any compensating advantage; and so it has been rejected (*Wilsher v Essex AHA* [1988] AC 1074). The proportional approach makes it easier for the harm-sufferer to recover something, but reduces the risk that the harm-doer will have to pay out in full. It is followed in some cases. For example, if a solicitor negligently fails to begin a tort action in time so that the harm-sufferer's claim is unsuccessful, the harm-sufferer may be able to sue the solicitor for loss of the chance of winning damages. If the harm-sufferer can prove, on the balance of probabilities, that if the solicitor had not been negligent the action would have gone ahead with a significant chance of success, damages against the solicitor will be assessed as a percentage of what would have been recovered if the action that was never started had been successful, depending on the estimated chance that that action would have succeeded. In one case, however, the House of Lords refused to allow a claimant to recover damages proportional to the chance that a medical procedure, which he had been negligently denied, would have been successful and would have prevented him developing a medical condition (*Hotson v East Berks HA* [1987] AC 750). It is not clear how this difference of approach should be explained.

Why is the basic rule of liability all-or-nothing rather than proportionality to risk? A practical answer to this question may be that a thoroughgoing system of liability proportional to risk would be exceedingly difficult to operate because in very many cases, the statistical evidence necessary to calculate risks in a mathematically accurate way would not be available. Theoretically, the answer, I believe, is that tort law seeks to strike a fair balance between the interest of the harm-sufferer in not being interfered with and the interest of the defendant in freedom of action. The rule, of no liability below a threshold and full liability above it, is a rough but not obviously unfair compromise between the competing interests of the two parties. If that is right, why is the burden of proof under the all-or-nothing approach set at the balance of probabilities? The best answer may simply be that the balance-of-probabilities standard is intuitively attractive as a minimum; that it would be difficult to describe clearly in words any particular threshold higher than 'balance of probabilities' and lower than 'beyond reasonable doubt' (the criminal burden); and that to use a figure (such as 75 per cent) would be pointless given that the statistical information necessary to arrive at such a figure would rarely, if ever, be available. Furthermore (as already noted), in practice, because reliable statistical evidence will usually be lacking, what matters is not whether the balance-of-probabilities threshold has been reached but whether the court is satisfied that it has. This means that to meet the burden of proof, all the claimant can do is to bring before the court all the evidence they have supporting their case and hope that it will satisfy the court that the threshold (whatever it is) has been reached.

ASSESSMENT OF DAMAGES

A third reason why bringing a tort claim to court may be very costly lies in the legal rules about assessment of damages in personal injury cases.

In the typical tort case, damages 'compensate' for damage caused by the harm-doer to the harm-sufferer. Recall that 'damage' is injury—physical, mental and so on—resulting from an interference with a protected interest. In some cases, 'restitutionary' damages may be awarded to strip the harm-doer of some benefit acquired by the tortious conduct. Very rarely, damages may be awarded in cases where the harm-doer causes no damage but merely interferes with a protected interest—for instance, by entering someone's land without authorisation. Such damages are called 'nominal' or 'vindicatory'. They are (relatively) small in amount and simply mark the fact that a protected interest has been interfered with. In very rare cases, where the court considers the interference trivial or the harm-sufferer undeserving, they may be called 'contemptuous'.

At the other extreme, 'punitive' or 'exemplary' damages are occasionally awarded to mark the court's disapproval of the harm-doer's conduct because, for instance, it was planned and deliberate, showing disrespect for the harm-sufferer. Punitive damages will be substantial and are typically awarded in cases where the tortious conduct has also caused significant damage. Most commonly, however, damages are awarded, and awarded only, to compensate for damage caused by the harm-doer's tortious conduct.

A confusing variety of terms are used to refer to damage. The word 'loss' is used in phrases such as 'economic loss' and 'compensation for loss'; 'injury' is used in phrases such as 'personal injury'; 'harm' is used in phrases such as 'mental harm'. In this discussion of compensation, all these terms can be treated as synonyms for 'damage'. (But remember that elsewhere we have distinguished between 'harm' and 'damage' (page 36–7). In this usage, all torts cause harm, but not all torts cause damage.)

Damage is what is compensated for. The remedy of compensation for damage is, confusingly, called 'damages'. The phrase 'heads of damage' refers to the various types of damage for which compensation can be given. The phrase 'the measure of damages' refers to the formulae used to calculate damages 'under' the various heads. The phrase 'quantum of damages' refers to the amount of compensation awarded. The process of calculating the quantum of damages is referred to as 'assessment of damages'. Perhaps the most important distinction in this mass of terminology is that between 'damage' and 'damages': damages (plural, the remedy) compensate for damage (singular, the consequence(s) of the tort).

The rules about assessment of compensatory tort damages for personal injury are extremely complex and technical; and it is, fortunately, unnecessary to describe them in detail here. It will be enough to provide an outline that will help the reader to understand why assessment of damages can be very costly in time and resources. (For more detail see Cane 2013, chapter 6).

Heads of Damage for Personal Injuries

There are various 'heads of damage'. These include:

— Loss of income in the past (before the date when the damages are being assessed). For example, a person in work who is injured in a road accident might unable to work for a period and will be entitled to be compensated for loss of the wages which would have been payable if they had been able to work during that period.
— Loss of income in the future (after the date when the damages are being assessed). For example, a working person may be so badly injured in a road accident that they will never be able to work again. Such a person could be compensated in tort not only for 'past loss of income' but also for 'future loss of income' in the period when they would normally have been expected to go on working if they had not been injured.
— Medical and related expenses incurred in the past that would not have been incurred but for the tort.
— Medical and related expenses that will probably be incurred in the future that would not have been incurred but for the tort.
— 'Non-pecuniary (or 'non-financial') loss' such as 'pain and suffering', distress, anxiety and inconvenience; and 'loss of amenities' such as the use of a limb.

Damages 'under' each of these heads of damage are designed to compensate the harm-sufferer in money for the actual or hypothetical (expected) deterioration in their position as a result of the tort.

Compensation in Theory

Assessing the quantum of compensatory damages is a complicated and technical process that may be very costly. This is partly because in theory, in every tort case, damages are to be assessed taking account of all the facts relevant to the individual claimant's pre-injury and post-injury condition, often for many years into the future.

The concept of compensation can be unpacked into two separate principles: the '100 per cent principle' and the 'standard-of-living principle'. The 100 per cent principle says that compensation must be 'full'. This principle is most easily applied to past financial losses—they have already occurred, and they can be assessed reasonably accurately by taking evidence of market values of goods and services. The full compensation principle is less easily applied to future financial losses because of the uncertainties inherent in predicting the future; but the difficulties are practical rather than theoretical. The principle is least easily applied in relation to non-pecuniary losses (whether past or future), which relate to things that have no market value. In this context, 'full' compensation is usually interpreted to mean 'fair' compensation—that is, an amount that seems large enough to recognise the seriousness of what has been suffered but not so large that it seems 'unfair' to the harm-doer. In practice, in personal injury cases, damages for non-pecuniary loss are calculated according to a quite detailed set of guidelines published by the Judicial Studies Board (the body responsible for the continuing education of judges). These guidelines set an upper limit of around £337,700 for cases involving the most serious injuries such as quadriplegia and severe brain damage. Although some consider this figure too low, its rationale, perhaps, is that for most people, such a sum is a lot of money, and large enough to acknowledge the wrong done and the injury suffered. The guidelines describe various categories of injury (such as loss of an arm, or disfigurement, or brain damage) and specify for each category a range (say, £20,000–£50,000). The amount awarded in any particular case is decided according to the seriousness of the claimant's injuries within the relevant category.

The second principle of compensation is the 'standard-of-living principle'. It dictates that compensation for pecuniary loss should reflect the claimant's pre-tort financial position in life. The tort system does not redress inequalities in the distribution of income and resources in society. Rather, by awarding compensation related to the claimant's pre-tort standard of living, it ameliorates disruption to their lives and life-plans (Goodin 1995, chapter 11; also Goodin 1989). The basic principle of compensation in tort law is restorative or corrective, not re-distributional. The standard-of-living principle implies not only that compensation for loss of income should be 'earnings-related' but also that someone who, as a result of a tort, is unable to continue to do productive but unpaid work consisting of familial caring (such as cleaning a house and cooking) should be compensated for the value of that work. Compensation can also be awarded to an injured claimant representing the value of nursing and other domestic services made necessary by the tort and provided gratuitously by a family member or friend, whether or not the carer gave up paid work in order to be able to provide the care.

There are types of situation in which a person held liable in tort may end up paying less than these two principles dictate. First, if the claimant has been contributorily negligent, the amount payable by the defendant may be reduced to reflect the claimant's responsibility for the loss suffered. Second, where two or more harm-doers are held liable for the same loss, although each is liable to compensate the victim in full, as between themselves they may each be required to 'contribute' a proportion of the damages reflecting the responsibility of each for the damage inflicted.

Compensation in Practice

Normally, damages are assessed once only, once and for all, in respect of past, actual and future, likely damage. Suppose that a young person is tortiously injured in a way that will have permanent detrimental effects on their health, lifestyle and earning capacity. When awarding tort damages the court will usually assess damages as a single 'lump sum' to compensate for all past and future damage resulting from the tort. The assumption is that the claimant will invest this lump sum to produce a continuing income for as long as it is needed. Courts rarely order that damages be paid in the form of 'periodical payments' or a 'pension'. Originally, this approach was probably adopted because courts had no way of supervising compliance with such an order.

The result is that in assessing damages the court must normally speculate about the future in the attempt to calculate a lump sum that will, as nearly as possible, compensate for future damage. Since the purpose of compensatory damages is to put the claimant into the position they would have been in if the tort had not occurred, the court must speculate not only about what their life will be like as an injured person (including, for instance whether their health will deteriorate further in the future as a result of the injuries), but also about the position they would have been in if they had not been injured. Speculation is required not only about the claimant's health and other personal circumstances, but also about matters such as inflation, and tax and interest rates (which affect the amount of income which any lump sum award will be able to generate). This once-for-all rule means that the assessment of damages is a hit and-miss affair. Indeed, in very many cases it authorises awards of damages that inevitably either overcompensate or undercompensate, if only because the future is impossible to predict with complete accuracy. To make matters worse, claimants who receive large amounts in respect of long-term injuries carry a heavy burden in investing the damages wisely to produce the projected continuing income.

The once-for-all rule is one of the main reasons why assessing compensatory damages can be very costly. It involves speculation about various factors, the operation and effect of which may be extremely unclear and open to significant disagreement. In serious cases, such disagreements may result in large differences between what the claimant thinks will be needed to provide full, standard-of-living compensation and what the defendant considers will be sufficient. The larger the sums at stake, the more sense it makes to devote considerable time and resources to resolving the disagreements. Conversely, the smaller the sums in issue the less worthwhile it is to spend time and money arguing about the 'correct' amount of compensation. Better for the defendant to pay what the claimant asks for than to spend a large amount to secure a small reduction in the compensation. Conversely for the claimant.

4. SETTLEMENT

Most personal-injury tort claims are settled out of court without judicial involvement, by negotiation and agreement between a claimant represented by a lawyer (who may be acting on instructions from an insurer, such as a company from which the claimant has purchased insurance against the risk of having to litigate) and a defendant represented by a lawyer acting on instructions from a liability insurer. Perhaps the main reason why most personal-injury tort claims are settled is that applying the rules of tort law according to their terms may be very expensive relative to the amount of compensation claimed and is not, anyway, required in order to make a lawful settlement contract that could, in the last resort, be enforced by the power of the state. It follows that most personal-injury tort claims are not resolved by an application of tort doctrine to the claim by a court but rather by a negotiatied agreement between the parties about how tort doctrine will be applied. It follows, further, that in the typical case, the agreed application of the doctrine may be different from what the official application would have been had that case gone to court.

Putting the point bluntly, a defendant may agree to pay compensation despite lack of proof, to the requisite standard, of negligence or causation; or may agree to pay an amount of compensation greater than application by a court of the rules of assessment of damages would require. Conversely, a claimant may agree to withdraw a claim because of inability to prove negligence or causation, even though further investigation could have produced evidence that would have satisfied a court on these issues; or may agree to accept compensation less than an official application of the rules of assessment of damages would justify. From one point of view, the possible gap between the terms of a settlement agreement and the likely outcome of an official application of tort doctrine might seem unfair. Surely 'justice' requires proper application of the doctrine in every case? On the other hand, however valuable 'justice' may be, it is not costless (or, we might say, 'priceless'). In the end, doing justice must compete, for limited social resources, with healthcare, education and other highly valued social goods. At some point, the potential, aggregate social cost of doing 'tort justice according to the law' in every case would outweigh the expected, aggregate, social benefits. In the individual case, social justice may require being satisfied with agreement 'in the shadow of the law' as opposed to judicial decision 'according to law'. In court, tort doctrine determines the outcome; out of court it is merely influential.

Nevertheless, the settlement process certainly has a dark side. In an extremely influential article (Galanter 1974), US scholar Marc Galanter distinguished between participants in legal processes on the basis of whether they were 'one-shotters' or 'repeat-players'. The typical personal injury claimant is a one-shotter, while the typical defendant—in the guise of a liability insurer—is a repeat-player. Galanter's basic argument was that repeat-player defendants have various (unfair) advantages over one-shotter claimants in the litigation process. Galanter's analysis has provided the conceptual framework for academic studies of the tort settlement process over the past 40 years; and, in their authors' opinions anyway, they have tended to confirm Galanter's thesis. By contrast, those who argue that we now live in a 'blame' or 'compensation' culture maintain that developments over that period have turned the tables, and that the advantage now lies with claimants to an extent that threatens economic prosperity and the value of personal responsibility. Where the 'truth' lies is partly a matter of perspective and interpretation; and the opposing sides of the debate predictably argue for very different 'reforms' of the tort system. In fact, we do not know enough about how the settlement process works to decide which of these perspectives is nearer the truth.

So what do we know? In the typical personal injury case, settlement involves a largely unregulated process of bargaining between the harm-doer and the harm-sufferer conducted on their behalf by lawyers (for more see Cane 2013, chapter 10). The settlement process involves what economists call a 'bilateral monopoly': the claimant can 'sell' their claim to only one potential buyer—the insurer—and the insurer can 'buy' the claim from only one potential seller—the claimant. The claimant cannot, as it were, 'shop around' to get good value for the claim. The length and course of the bargaining process depend on various factors: the efficiency, skill and experience of the claimant's representative; the time needed to collect evidence; whether it is necessary to wait and see how the claimant's medical condition will develop before assessing damages; the number of issues in dispute; and whether the parties and their representatives take a confrontational or a co-operative approach to the settlement process. Typically, defendants and insurers have less to lose by delay than claimants.

The respective aims of the defendant and the defendant's insurer in the settlement process are usually the same: to minimise the amount paid out to the claimant. For this reason, insurers are well-placed to exploit to their own advantage any inexperience or ineptitude on the part of the claimant's representative, any weaknesses in the claimant's case and any uncertainties in the law. By contrast, the interests of the claimant and their representative may be in conflict: the best move for the representative may be to settle quickly, while the client's best interest may lie in pressing the claim and possibly commencing court proceedings to put pressure on the defendant. Rejection of an insurer's first offer commonly leads to a second, increased offer being made, and in some cases the process can be repeated several times. However, in most cases, the first offer is accepted. The difficulty and uncertainties of litigation and fear of lengthy further negotiations are, no doubt, potent factors in explaining the high level of acceptance of first offers. Many personal injury claimants will have had no previous experience of making a legal claim, and may find the whole process bewildering or even frightening. The emotional stress generated by having been injured, and then by having to engage in disagreeable haggling, often produces a desire to settle as quickly as possible, even if at an unreasonably low figure. The insurer, who is experienced in the process and emotionally uninvolved, can better afford to 'sit it out'.

As for the amounts of compensation received as a result of settlement negotiations, there are some grounds for believing that in cases of minor injury (the great majority), claimants tend to recover a larger proportion of what a strict application of the rules of assessment of damages would require. Intuitively, we would expect smaller claims to be contested less vigorously by insurers, both as to liability and assessment of damages, than larger ones, because the smaller the claim, the greater its nuisance value; or, in other words, the greater the likelihood that the cost of contesting it will be greater than the amount of the claim. There is no necessary relationship between the size of a claim and how difficult and complex it is in legal terms. Large claims may be very simple and small claims very complex. But the smaller the claim, the more likely that resisting it will not be financially worthwhile. Insurers do not like large claims and will investigate and resist them with vigour. On the other hand, however weak the claimant's case, it may still pay the defendant to settle a small claim rather than to fight. For reasons of cost and administrative efficiency, insurers typically settle low-value claims on the basis of rules-of-thumb—such as that rear-end accidents are always the fault of the following driver—rather than a thorough investigation of the issue of fault. Such rules-of-thumb are not only simpler and cheaper to apply than the legal concept of fault, but they also tend to be more favourable to claimants than strict rules of law. In practice, few claims are totally worthless so long as there is at least some room for argument about fault. This explains the fact that most claims result in the payment of some compensation.

8

Politics

KI 6: Tort law is political

1. THE POLITICAL FOUNDATIONS
OF TORT LAW

Your first reaction to this odd-sounding claim may well be to protest that 'law is one thing and politics quite another': tort law should be a politics-free zone. You might concede that some areas of law are obviously and, perhaps rightly, political: social security law, for example. Even so, you might insist that tort law is different: it is and should be about the rights and duties of individuals in their dealings with one another. 'Playing politics' with tort law (some might say) is deplorable. This sort of argument has become very popular in recent years. Amongst tort scholars, probably its most famous proponent is Ernest Weinrib (Weinrib 2012a, 2012b). He argues that tort law is concerned with 'corrective justice', not 'distributive justice'; and that 'distributive justice is the home of the political' (Weinrib 2012a, 210). Others have similarly argued that tort law is about 'rights and duties', not 'policy' (for example, Stevens 2007). Some people argue that because tort law is primarily about correcting individual wrongs and protecting individual rights, it is better for tort law to be made by courts than by Parliament because courts make law in the process of (and as a by-product) of correcting wrongs and protecting rights whereas Parliament makes law 'politically', without regard to individual claims and remedies.

What is 'playing politics', and what is objectionable about it? Imagine an opposition leader who attacks the government's public spending record at the scene of an apartment block fire in which people are killed and

injured. He or she may—fairly or unfairly—be accused of playing political games. The appropriate reaction at such a time, critics might say,
would be to concentrate on the personal plight of the victims and their
loved ones, and leave the political point-scoring for later. At the bottom
of such a reaction, I think, is the idea that the proper focus of political
activity is on society and groups, not on individuals—on the overall costs
and benefits of decisions, not their personal impact on winners and losers. We don't want our politicians to lose their nerve because decisions
that are good for society produce some personal tragedies. At the same
time, we don't want our politicians comforting a policy's victims with
nothing more than the thought that all government decisions produce
losers as well as winners.

The main business of politics is the distribution among the members
of society of the benefits and burdens of living together. In this sense, the
politics (or the 'policies') of (personal-injury) tort law concern the way
the benefits it provides (remedies) and the costs it imposes (liability) are
distributed amongst social groups—tort law's winners and losers, if you
like. In other words, the politics (and policies) of tort law are not about
how individual tort claims are resolved, but rather about the general
rules and principles that determine how individual claims are dealt with.
A good illustration is the classic case of *Donoghue v Stevenson* [1932]
AC 562. That case changed tort law. Before the decision, tort law would
not allow a person injured by a defective product to sue the manufacturer. The Court decided that in future, it should. Before the decision,
consumers of defective products were tort law's losers; but after the decision they were its winners and manufacturers became its new losers.
Tort law, we might say, does 'justice according to law'. 'Justice' refers to
the 'correction' of harm in individual cases, and 'law' refers to the rules
that determine how the cost of (correcting) harm is 'distributed'. Many
resist the idea that tort law is political because they focus on how tort law
applies in individual cases and neglect the general rules that determine
how individual cases are dealt with.

'Well', you might reply, 'I can see easily enough that social security law
is about distributing benefits and burdens rather than correcting wrongs,
but I'm not so sure about tort law.' Social security law seems obviously
about distributive justice because it is designed to *re*-distribute financial
wealth from members of one *group*, merely because they have it, to members of another *group*, merely because they need it. It is not concerned
with justice between individuals. However, it is a mistake to think about

distribution solely or primarily in terms of *re*distribution, because redistribution involves departure from a status quo that is itself a distribution. Law doesn't have to be redistributive to be distributive. It's also a mistake to think of redistribution as necessarily involving transfer from rich to poor. For instance, consumption taxes typically fall more heavily on the poor than the rich (they are 'regressive'), and we may easily think of awards of tort damages as transferring resources from harm-doers to harm-sufferers regardless of their relative wealth. Indeed, a fundamental criticism that is sometimes made of tort law is precisely that it disregards the relative wealth of the two parties and is, generally, regressive in its effect. This is because it is funded by liability insurance, the cost of which is related to the risk that the insured will be held liable in tort, not the insured's wealth; but its benefits are related to the wealth of the harm-sufferer. The more you earn, the more you get out of the tort system, regardless of how much you put in. By contrast, both the funding of the social security system—by general, and broadly 'progressive'—taxation, and the benefits it provides—typically flat-rate or income-related—take account of the wealth of contributors on the one hand and beneficiaries on the other.

So we do not have to look too hard to get a picture of tort law as a mechanism for (re)distribution of wealth funded on the basis of risk. From this perspective, tort law, like social security law, is a set of rules and principles about entitlement to benefits and a set of rules about obligations to contribute to the funding of those benefits. The tort system and the social security system are both about distributing wealth amongst social groups. What primarily distinguishes tort law from social security law is not its basic character but the details of its benefit and funding rules. If, as most would concede, the benefit and funding rules of the social security system matters are of political concern, the benefit and funding rules of the tort system are also of political concern. The fact that many of the most important rules of tort law are made by courts, not Parliament, does not deprive them of their political salience.

2. FIVE FACES OF THE POLITICS OF TORT LAW

In this section I will say something about each of five strands in political debates about tort law. What I mean by political debates are debates about how the rules and principles of tort law should be designed or changed rather than debates about the way tort law is applied in individual cases. They are the politics of regulation, the politics of compensation, the politics of responsibility, the politics of law-making and the politics of claiming.

THE POLITICS OF REGULATION

Regulation is about using legal rules and institutions 'instrumentally' to influence our behaviour as potential harm-doers and self-harmers, and to minimise the incidence of harm caused by such behaviour. The idea that tort law might be used in this way became extremely popular in the United States in the 1960s and 1970s and now underpins the way many US lawyers think about tort law. Starting from the position that 'the time has come for a full re-examination of what we want a system of accident law to accomplish and for an analysis of how different approaches to accidents would accomplish our goals', and that 'the principal function of accident law is to' minimise the social costs of accidents, Guido Calabresi suggested that instead of distributing the cost of harm resulting from road accidents to the party whose tortious conduct caused the harm, the law should distribute the cost to the party who could have avoided it most cheaply (Calabresi 1970). It is implicit in this approach that allocating the costs of harm on the basis of the relative capacity of the harm-doer and the harm-sufferer to avoid harm cheaply, rather than on the basis of their relative fault in causing the harm, would produce a more desirable distribution of the costs and benefits of social life associated with motor traffic. This is a political argument.

The practical implications of Calabresi's recommendations are radical. Giving effect to the cheapest-cost-avoider principle would, as he recognised, require the abolition, rather than merely the reform, of tort law, and the introduction of an entirely different system designed to identify cheapest cost avoiders. Where the cheapest cost avoider was the harm-sufferer, that person would bear the costs of the accident. If it was some other person, the principle would require that other person to pay the costs of the accident but, unlike tort law, it would not necessarily require the costs to be paid to the harm-sufferer personally. However, this sort of regulatory approach to accident law has not, in fact, generated radical reform proposals, even though it is pervasive in the US and has been popularised in Hollywood docudramas such as *A Civil Action* (1998) and *Erin Brockovich* (2000). In these stories we see tort law being used as an alternative to 'command and control regulation' involving, for instance, enforcement of workplace safety regulations and environmental quality standards, ultimately, by a system of prosecution and penalties rather than individual tort claims.

The predominant ideology of English personal injuries law is not regulatory, and there are relatively few strong advocates of using tort law primarily for regulatory purposes. The regulatory approach lacks support partly because empirical studies provide little evidence that tort law can make a significant contribution to the minimisation of accident costs; and many believe that the distributional consequences, of substituting the cheapest-cost-avoider principle for the fault principle currently embodied in tort law, would be unacceptable. For such people, the whole (political) point of 'accident law' is to correct wrongs, not to reduce accident costs. The disagreement is fundamental and political.

THE POLITICS OF COMPENSATION

This leads us on to the second strand in political debates about tort law: the politics of compensation. In contrast to Calabresi, the Canadian legal scholar, Terence Ison, began by assuming that 'compensation' of harm-sufferers, rather than accident-cost-minimisation, was the prime function of accident law (Ison 1967). Ison looked carefully at tort law and found it seriously deficient as a mechanism for compensating victims of personal injuries. The practical implications of his approach were just as radical as those of Calabresi's. But unlike Calabresi, Ison followed through, and made a practical proposal for replacing tort law with a 'no-fault' system of compensation based on the provision of social-security-type payments for 'diseases and violent injuries causing disablement and death', regardless of whether they were the result of anyone's tortious conduct. The 1970s was the heyday of this compensatory approach to accident law. In 1974 a system, broadly of the sort Ison proposed, was introduced in New Zealand covering most accidental injuries. In England, a Royal Commission, which reported in 1978, recommended the enactment of a system of no-fault compensation for road accidents, but this never happened. In the 1970s and 1980s many no-fault compensation schemes were put in place around the world, mostly limited to road accidents or medical mishaps. However, by the late 1980s, the move to no-fault had run out of steam, and by the 1990s the political climate had become distinctly hostile to the sort of communitarian solutions to 'the problem of personal injuries' that had been favoured by reform-minded lawyers since the 1960s.

In England in the twenty-first century, total or even partial replacement of tort law with no-fault alternatives for dealing with personal injuries is politically inconceivable. The tort system has become an entrenched feature of the 'political economy' of personal-injuries law (Cane 2007). In the 1970s political debates about personal-injury law focused on how to replace tort law. Now, they focus on how to live with it while solving what are considered its most significant problems.

THE POLITICS OF RESPONSIBILITY

Tort law redistributes financial resources from harm-doers to harm-sufferers. It also distributes risk between potential harm-doers and potential harm-sufferers: causing harm by the conduct of risky activities is the trigger of redistribution of resources through tort law. Tort liability for personal injuries is liability based on responsibility for the creation of risks of personal injury—but only certain risks. The rules and principles of tort law specify the sorts of risks that can attract liability if, and when, they result in harm to another. Responsibility for preventing harm caused by such risks is allocated to those who undertake risky activities. So far as concerns risks that fall outside the scope tort law, potential harm-sufferers must look out for themselves—in other words, they must take responsibility for their own safety. The politics of responsibility are the politics of risk. Just as we can ask the political question of whether resources are (re)distributed fairly, can also ask whether risks—and responsibility—are distributed fairly. Tort law (re)distributes resources fairly if, but only if, it distributes risks fairly. This is the domain of the politics of responsibility.

The politics of regulation, like the politics of responsibility, is concerned with distribution of risks; and the politics of compensation, like the politics of responsibility, is concerned with redistribution of resources. The politics of responsibility is distinctive in tying together these two concerns with risks on the one hand and resources on the other. Tort law is doubly distributive, doubly political: it distributes risks *and* resources.

The historical trajectory of the politics of responsibility over the past 50 years is nicely illustrated by the work of Patrick Atiyah. In *Accidents, Compensation and the Law* (Atiyah 1970), he argued for the abolition of tort liability for personal injuries first on the basis that it was an inefficient regulatory tool; and second on the ground not only that as a compensation mechanism it was hugely expensive, but also that it distributed resources unfairly between various groups of harm-sufferers. His reform proposal (similarly to Ison's) focused on the second of these criticisms and more-or-less ignored the first. He recommended an extension of the industrial-injuries component of the UK social security system to include sickness and disability however caused, to be funded by increased social security contributions.

Almost 30 years later, in *The Damages Lottery* (Atiyah 1997), Atiyah once again argued for the abolition of tort law as a means of dealing with the social problems of personal injuries. However, this time his reform proposal was framed in terms of personal responsibility rather than compensation. The main problem with tort law, he argued, was that it had developed a bias in favour of harm-sufferers at the expense of harm-doers, thereby unfairly distributing risks of harm, and resources, between the two groups. In the process, it had created a 'blame culture' in which, typically, people's first reaction to adversity was to blame someone else. In fact, however, what had changed since the 1970s was not tort law but the political culture in which it operated. In the 1980s, Thatcherite neo-liberals began to paint not only the social security system (which Atiyah had championed in the earlier book), but also the tort system, as sources of dependency. As much as possible, they argued, people should take responsibility for their own health and safety and not look to either the social security system or the tort system for relief when things go wrong. In this spirit, Atiyah proposed the replacement of the tort system of liability funded by liability insurance with a new regime in which potential harm-sufferers would insure themselves against suffering harm using 'first-party' or 'loss' insurance rather than 'third-party' or 'liability' insurance.

THE POLITICS OF LAW-MAKING

At bottom, Calabresi, Ison and Atiyah were all 'abolitionists'. They thought that tort law was such a deficient mechanism for dealing with the social problems of personal injuries that they favoured its replacement with a regime that would better achieve whatever each considered to be the main goal of tort law, whether that related to accident prevention, compensation or responsibility. An alternative to wholesale abolition of tort law is incremental reform. For instance, to promote the regulatory goal, reformers may favour greater use of punitive damages to give potential wrong-doers stronger messages than liability to compensate by itself can deliver; or making it easier for large groups of harm-sufferers to band together to claim against the manufacturer of a defective product or an industrial polluter, reducing individual costs and generating publicity. Proponents of the compensation goal have tended to focus on persuading law-makers to create new heads of damages and to increase levels of damages. One neo-liberal response is to argue for 'ceilings', 'thresholds' and 'caps' on damages designed, particularly, to discourage low-value claims that are disproportionately costly to process, and to encourage people to find alternatives to tort claims to protect them against risks of very serious personal injury.

This brings us to the fourth aspect of the politics of tort law—the politics of law-making. Parliament makes law, but so do courts. Parliament makes law by enacting 'statutes'; courts make 'common law'. Common law is (typically) made in the process of deciding cases; statutes (typically) make no reference to individual cases. Traditionally, tort law has been made by courts, not Parliaments. However, since the mid-nineteenth century, the volume of statutory tort law has increased greatly. In the English system of law, the more radical a proposed change to the law, the more likely it will (have to) be made by Parliament rather than the courts, by politicians rather than judges, by statute rather than common law. Abolitionists are, of necessity, tolerant of wholesale Parliamentary interventions, whereas some reformers argue that because tort law has traditionally been made by judges, Parliament should make tort law only when the courts are unwilling or unable to do so. A preference for common-law over statutory tort law affects the extent and types of changes that can be made to it.

Politics is about the distribution of risks and harms, but also about the distribution of power, including law-making power. The politics of law-making are the politics of power-distribution. In Australia near the turn of the century it was a subject of vigorous political debate (Cane 2003). A government committee was established to recommend statutory changes to personal-injury tort law to make it harder for harm-sufferers to win tort claims. The premise was that the balance of responsibility between potential harm-sufferers and potential harm-doers had swung too far in favour of the former. With a view to redressing the balance, the committee proposed various changes to tort rules concerned with tortious conduct, causation and defences. One of the arguments used by those opposed to the changes was that the judges could achieve the desired result themselves without the intervention of the legislature, and should be left to do so. This could be done either by incremental adjustment of relevant rules or, even, by different application of the existing rules in individual cases without any explicit adjustment.

Arguments such as this are possible because in the English legal system (and the Australian) there are two distinct sources of law—statutes made by Parliaments and common law made by courts. Neither legislatures nor courts by themselves have the resources to make all the rules that need to be made to satisfy the (insatiable) social demand for law. The politics of law-making concern the distribution of law-making power between legislatures and courts. Because legislatures and courts respectively are staffed quite differently and follow quite different law-making procedures, the choice between them can generate considerable (political) disagreement and contention.

THE POLITICS OF CLAIMING

In England, none of the political issues so far canvassed in this chapter has received much attention in the past 20 or 30 years. Instead of concern with the goals, content, and even the very existence, of tort law, the focus has been on tort claiming and 'access to justice'. Processing tort claims both in and out of court costs money and, as we noted in Chapter 7, can be very expensive and time-consuming. Unlike paying compensation, which transfers resources from harm-doer to harm-sufferer, claiming consumes resources in meeting the cost of legal (and other related) professional services and of the court system. In the 1980s in England, the basic legal rule was that the legal costs incurred by the successful party would be paid by the unsuccessful party, who would also pay their own legal costs. In practice, the legal costs of defending a personal-injury tort claim were typically borne by the defendant's liability insurer, who also had to pay the claimant's costs if the claim succeeded. A significant proportion of personal-injury claimants were entitled to (means-tested) taxpayer-funded 'legal aid' (a form of social security payment) to cover their legal costs. If the claim was successful, the claimant was typically required to pay something back to the legal aid authorities. If the claim failed, normally nothing was payable. A claimant who did not qualify for legal aid might have insurance to cover legal costs ('legal expenses insurance'); otherwise they would have to carry the costs in the hope of winning and receiving an 'award of costs' against the defendant. In practice, legal aid was critical to the operation of the tort system.

In the 1990s, two concerns began to dominate discussion of the processing of personal-injury claims (mostly by settlement out of court): the funding of claims, and the high cost, in time and money, of settlement out-of-court and, very occasionally, proceedings in court. The full story is long and complicated, but the main outlines can be briefly sketched. First, beginning in the late 1990s, the legal rules of court-based claiming procedure (which provide the structural framework for settlement negotiations) were overhauled with the aim of reducing the cost of settling standard claims (Sorabji 2014). Second, in the name of reducing public spending, legal aid was gradually made unavailable for personal-injury claims. Put in its place was the 'conditional-fee arrangement' under which lawyers could provide services to claimants on a 'no-win, no-fee basis', thus relieving them of the burden of paying costs upfront, and of paying costs at all if the claim failed. This fundamental change in the funding of legal services gave rise to a new industry—legal services broking by what became known as 'claims management companies' (CMCs). These entities, that typically operate on a no-win, no-fee basis, arrange for personal-injury claimants the various services—of solicitors, medical experts, litigation insurers and so on—needed to achieve a settlement of the claim. One result of these funding changes was that the annual number of road-accident, personal-injury claims, especially small claims, rose dramatically after 2005 (Cane 2013, 260–66).

The availability and cost of legal services are political issues about the distribution of the burdens and benefits of social life. They are an inextricable part of the story of tort law because without legal services there would probably be very few, if any, tort claims and tort would be much less used to settle disputes. As has been made clear throughout this book, resolving disputes is certainly not tort doctrine's only, or even its most important, use, but it is probably its most visible.

9

Uses

KI 7: Tort law 'has its uses'

Like a knife safely stored in block or drawer, tort doctrine confined to the books is inert, waiting to be brought to life by use. Lawyers often talk about 'law's functions' or 'law's purposes', as if law were a person. I prefer to say that law is made by people for certain purposes and to perform certain functions, and that once made, it is available for people to use for those purposes and to perform those functions. The purposes are those of people, for whom law has its uses and functions.

It may be possible to use law for purposes other than those that its makers had in mind. The possible uses of law are limited only by the imagination and ingenuity of its users. Some uses of legal power may themselves be tortious (McBride and Bagshaw 2015, chapter 25); but subject to such legal constraints, law is available for any use that can practically be made of it. Like knives, law is more useful for some jobs than others. Criticism of tort law and recommendations for its reform or abolition are often based in its alleged inefficacy and inefficiency in doing the jobs we use it for.

Some of the functions that people most often use tort law for are:

— Guiding conduct.
— Allocating risk.
— Remedying harm.
— Preventing harm.
— Punishing wrongdoing.
— Doing justice.
— Vindicating rights.

We will say something about each of these in turn.

1. GUIDING CONDUCT

As **KI 1** tells us, tort law is law. Law-in-general has uses that tort law shares. These include giving people guidance about how they may, ought and ought not to behave in their interactions with others, protecting certain interests, expressing disapproval of certain types of conduct and providing remedies for adverse effects, maintaining social order and promoting social cohesion by providing means of resolving disputes, and supplementing morality both by applying its general principles to particular circumstances and by providing socially acceptable and enforceable compromises between irreconcilably conflicting moral views. As was argued in Chapter 2, law's rich institutional resources may make it particularly useful compared with other less-institutionalised social normative systems.

Just how useful law can be in guiding conduct will depend, for instance, on how clear and precise its rules are, on the extent to which they are internally consistent, and how much people know about them. To the extent that law's usefulness depends on its institutional resources, the nature and quality of its institutions will be critical. For instance, the fact that courts are used so little for handling tort claims suggests that they are of very limited use in resolving tort disputes. In practice, the markets in insurance and legal services are much more useful. There is an important general point here. Few, if any, of the uses of law belong to it uniquely. For some purposes, law may be particularly useful but it is rarely, if ever, the only tool available for any particular use; and when law does not deliver, we may reach for other tools.

2. ALLOCATING RISK

As we saw in Chapter 4, tort law defines negligence as failure to take precautions against risks involved in human activities and conduct. Negligence is faulty creation of risks. Sometimes, non-faulty creation of risks can be tortious. When risky conduct results in damage, tort law allocates the risk by allocating the burden of bearing the cost of the damage. However, tort law sometimes allocates risk regardless of damage—for instance, when it defines trespass to land merely in terms of entering the land. By doing so, it allocates the risk of unauthorised entry to the entrant rather than the person in possession of the land.

By allocating risks, tort law gives effect to value judgements of law-makers about how risks ought to be allocated. As was argued in Chapter 8, decisions about how to allocate risk are political and social. However, the law may also allow individuals to agree amongst themselves to allocate risks differently than tort law does. The main vehicle used for this pur-pose is contract and, in particular, what are known as 'exclusion clauses' or 'exemption clauses' in contracts. The extent to which tort law's allocation of risk may be varied by contract is itself regulated by law. For instance (as we have seen), the law does not allow an exclusion clause to be used to shift the risk of negligently-caused personal injury from the harm-doer to the harm-sufferer (Unfair Contract Terms Act 1977, section 2(1)). Sometimes tort law itself provides for variation of its own initial allocation of risk. For example, tort law allows an occupier of land, in certain circum-stances, to post a notice warning visitors of a danger on the land. In the absence of the notice, the risk of damage resulting from the danger would be allocated to the occupier. The effect of the notice may be to reallocate the risk from the occupier to the visitor (but not in the case of negligently-caused personal injury: Unfair Contract Terms Act 1977, section 2(1)). Another way in which tort law allows reallocation of risks is through the defence of consent, which plays a crucial role, for instance, in shifting risks inherent in medical treatment from medical practitioners to patients (for more on this see, for example, Giliker and Beckwith 2011, 350–54).

3. REMEDYING DAMAGE

To the extent that tort law allocates the risk of damage to harm-doers, its institutional resources enable its use to provide remedies for the damage caused, typically in the form of compensatory damages. In Chapters 4 and 5 we saw how tort law allocates risks of damage (physical and mental injury, property damage, financial loss and so on). In Chapter 7 we discussed tort law's rules about compensatory damages (under the various 'heads of damages') and considered the role of courts—law's remedial institutions—in providing remedies (by exploring the settlement process). There is no need to review those discussions here.

How effective is tort law—doctrine and institutions—in remedying damage the risk of which the doctrine allocates to harm-doers? Considering that there are around a million, successful personal-injury tort claims in England each year and, no doubt, many more successful property-damage claims (for more on this see Cane 2013, 215–16), we might conclude that it is very effective. However, we do not know what proportion of the total number of potentially successful tort claims is represented by the body of claims that are made and succeed. We do know that in some contexts (such as accidents in the home), personal injury tort claims are very rarely made, despite the fact that more reported personal injuries result from accidents in the home than from accidents on the roads. It is reasonable to speculate that a significant proportion of personal injury caused in the home could, in theory, be the subject of a successful tort claim. However, for various reasons, such claims are rare (for more see Cane 2013, 206–07). Even amongst successful claims, there is some reason to think that in a significant proportion, especially of the more serious cases, the amount of damages actually received by the harm-sufferer is less than a strict application of tort doctrine would require (for more see Cane 2013, 282–84). As we saw in Chapter 7, this is because most claims are settled, and the outcome of settlement negotiations, while inevitably influenced by tort doctrine, may not represent a strict application of the rules.

The effectiveness of tort law in remedying damage depends not only on what proportion of potentially successful tort claims are made and succeed but also on how many successful claims ought not, on a strict application of tort doctrine, to have succeeded at all or to the extent that they did. Once again, because of the dynamics of the settlement process, there is reason to believe that some proportion of successful claims ought not to have succeeded and that, in a certain proportion of cases (especially the less serious), the damages paid were greater than a strict application of tort doctrine would justify.

Of course, whether such gaps between the doctrine and the practice are cause for criticism or concern depends on an assessment of the process as a whole, and its overall costs and benefits. The only point being made here is that the tort doctrine in the books is only the tip of the iceberg we call 'the tort system'.

4. PREVENTING DAMAGE

One of the purposes that tort law is most commonly employed to promote is 'deterrence' of tortious conduct and prevention of tortious damage. This is the realm of what, in Chapter 8, was referred to as the politics of regulation. Tort claimants often refer to this use of tort law when they say things like: 'it's not really the damages I want; I'm doing this to prevent the same thing happening to anyone else in the future'. The basic idea behind deterrence is that by establishing rules and standards of conduct and by attaching the remedy of damages (or, in the case of harm-sufferers, a reduction of damages) for failure to satisfy those standards and rules, the law can provide incentives for safe conduct and educate people about safety. Despite quite a lot of evidence, we know relatively little for certain about the deterrent effectiveness of tort law and tort liability. However, some general comments may be ventured.

The effectiveness of tort law as a deterrent depends partly on identifying, and imposing liability on, parties who are able, by taking care, to prevent damage occurring. The less we know about the causes of accidents and injuries, the less will we be able to use tort law as a means of establishing standards of safety. This problem is particularly acute in respect of illnesses and diseases, as opposed to traumatic personal injuries (Stapleton 1986, chapter 4). It is, no doubt, easier to deter deliberate conduct than it is to deter merely negligent conduct—for instance, easier to deter a surgeon from operating on a patient without his or her consent (by making consent available as a defence) than to deter the surgeon from making a negligent mistake in the course of the operation (by imposing a legal duty of care on surgeons). The risk of liability is no doubt a factor in deterring newspapers from publishing material that they realise might be defamatory (Barendt 1997). This doesn't mean that people cannot be deterred from negligent conduct. For instance, even if it is not feasible to deter a drunk from dangerous driving once behind the wheel, it may be possible to deter a person from drinking too much before driving.

Even so, there appear to be major barriers to the effective use of tort law and the risk of tort liability to prevent damage. Because most people know relatively little about tort law and will have had no direct experience of tort claiming, few may see tort liability as a serious possibility. Drivers, for instance, are perhaps more likely to take care out of concern for their own safety, or to avoid the risk of incurring a fine or driving disqualification, than by the risk of incurring tort liability. Professional pride, personal values, or potential loss of reputation and livelihood, may give surgeons stronger incentives to operate with care than tort law can provide. On the other hand, it is often argued that fear of tort liability may 'over-deter' professionals and cause them to take unnecessary and ineffective precautions (called 'defensive practice').

Tort law may also be used to encourage potential harm-sufferers to take care for their own safety by reducing damages on account of contributory negligence. However, if a person's instinct for self-preservation does not deter them from dangerous conduct it is, perhaps, unlikely that a denial of monetary or other assistance will do so. Criminal law may provide stronger incentives than tort law. The history of seat-belt usage provides a good illustration. During the period 1973–80 only about 30 per cent of drivers and front-seat passengers wore seat belts, despite the risk of receiving reduced damages if injured while not wearing a belt. In 1983, subject to limited exceptions, it became a criminal offence for a driver or front seat passenger not to wear a seat belt if provided. With the help of vigorous enforcement, the compliance rate rose to 95 per cent for cars and over 80 per cent for vans.

What is the likely impact of widespread, and often compulsory, liability insurance on the deterrent effect of tort law? It is universally accepted that liability insurance, although essential for realising tort law's compensatory potential, greatly reduces its deterrent efficacy. For instance, drivers who are not discouraged from taking careless risks by concern for their own safety or that of passengers in the car, nor by fear of the criminal law, nor by fear of being disqualified from driving, are not likely to be deterred by the risk of being sued in a tort action in which the damages will be paid by an insurance company. In some contexts, insurers attempt to counteract the negative incentive signals given by insurance (called 'moral hazard') by requiring insureds, under the terms of insurance policies, to take certain precautions and even checking up whether they have been taken. However, this is not done in the road accident context. Other techniques used by insurers to combat moral hazard include 'feature rating' (for instance, charging younger drivers higher premiums than older drivers), 'experience rating' (in the form of no-claims bonuses) and 'deductibles' (requiring the insured personally to pay a certain amount of the claim before the insurance kicks in). Unfortunately, although the theory underpinning such techniques is sound, there is no evidence that they have any significant effects on the incidence of accidents.

5. PUNISHING WRONGDOING

Punishing wrongdoers and expressing disapproval of wrongdoing is one of the main uses of the criminal law. The 'conventional wisdom' is that tort law should not be used to punish tortious wrongdoers. English tort law defines narrowly the circumstances in which 'punitive damages' are recoverable in a tort action (*Rookes v Barnard* [1964] AC 1129). Unless there is express statutory authority, punitive damages can be awarded in only two situations: first, where a person or body exercising governmental powers has been guilty of arbitrary, oppressive or unconstitutional conduct; and, second, where the wrongdoer has sought to make a profit out of the tort. The main arguments against punitive tort damages are that they amount to a criminal fine, but one that is imposed without the procedural safeguards for defendants which are built into the criminal process (such as proof beyond reasonable doubt); and that damages that do not represent any harm suffered by the claimant are a 'windfall', and so unjustifiable.

In the US, by contrast, punitive damages are sometimes awarded against corporate defendants, especially in unfair competition, product liability and environmental pollution cases. Some in this country have urged that punitive damages be more widely available in personal-injury actions, particularly those in which corporate or governmental defendants have been seriously and culpably inattentive to the safety of members of the public. The English Law Commission once recommended that punitive damages should be available in cases where the wrongdoer showed 'deliberate and outrageous disregard of the claimant's rights' (Law Commission 1997). Such a case could, in theory anyway, be a case of death or personal injury; but it is likely that such a rule would have no impact on the vast majority of personal-injury claims. On the other hand, it would make punitive damages available in some types of case in which they cannot currently be awarded: where, perhaps, an employer deliberately cuts corners on safety for the sake of profit.

6. DOING JUSTICE

Some people describe the chief purpose and use of tort law in terms of doing ('corrective') justice between wrong-doers and wrong-sufferers. By awarding compensation, it is said, the law aims to restore and redress the balance of fairness or justice that the wrong-doer has upset by tortious conduct. There is a huge modern literature on 'corrective justice' in tort law, and it contains many different definitions of the concept. However, the basic idea behind it is quite straightforward, and is fundamental to understanding tort law.

Every tort claim involves a harm-sufferer seeking some remedy from a harm-doer on the basis that the harm suffered was a result of tortious conduct by the harm-doer. The use of tort law for purposes other than doing corrective justice between harm-doers and harm-sufferers is necessarily constrained by the fact that tort liability depends on responsibility for harm to another. For instance, tort law compensates people for losses, but only if responsibility for those losses can be pinned on some other individual. We may seek to use tort law to reduce accident levels; but even if tort law is effective in reducing accidents, its effect is limited by the fact that it is only concerned with accidents that result in damage for which someone other than the harm-sufferer is responsible. We can use tort law to punish people, but only those responsible for tortiously harming others.

One way of putting this point is to say that doing corrective justice is an intrinsic, rather than a merely contingent, function of tort law because every tort has two main elements—protected interests of one person and harmful conduct of another that interferes with those interests—and in every tort claim a harm-sufferer claims a remedy from a harm-doer on the basis of the relationship between the wrong done and the harm suffered. Some people go further and argue that doing corrective justice is not merely one of the things tort law can be used for but rather what it does naturally. I would rather say that tort law's possible uses are limited and constrained by its 'corrective structure'.

7. PROVIDING VINDICATION

In cases where tort remedies are available regardless of whether the harm-doer has inflicted any damage on the harm-sufferer (where the tort is 'actionable per se'), we may say that tort law can be used to vindicate rights (Varuhas 2014).

In a more colloquial sense, making a successful tort claim may provide a sense of vindication or satisfaction through an award of compensatory or punitive damages. There is evidence that some tort claims against hospitals and doctors are a response to failure by the harm-doer to apologise rather than a desire to be compensated. In one case, the estate of a man shot by the police in mistake for a dangerous criminal was allowed to sue the police for 'battery' (ie for the shooting) even though the police had admitted liability for negligence and were prepared to settle out of court, and in full, his family's claim for financial loss, with the result that success in the battery claim would attract no additional compensation but, at most, an award of 'nominal damages' (*Ashley v Chief Constable of Sussex Police* [2008] 1 AC 962).

Tort claims that go to court may attract media attention that may be used to hold wrongdoers publicly accountable. However, most tort actions attract very little publicity even if they go to trial; and (as we saw in Chapter 7), the vast majority are settled out of court by private agreement. Settlement agreements typically contain clauses by which the claimant agrees not to publicise the grounds or terms of the settlement. Furthermore, settlements are typically made 'without admission of liability' on the part of the harm-doer, who may prefer settlement to trial precisely in order to prevent the facts of the claim being publicised. Another barrier to use of tort law for vindication is the rule that if the harm-doer (or the harm-doer's insurer) offers sufficient compensation to the claimant by way of settlement of the claim, but the claimant rejects the offer and insists on a trial out of a desire for public vindication, they will normally have to pay the costs of the hearing (Cane 2013, 277–79).

It has been argued that tort law can be used as a public grievance mechanism similar to a complaint to an ombudsman, especially in cases against public authorities or large corporations (such as drug companies or transport undertakings) whose actions have caused widespread damage or injury to many people (Linden and Feldthusen 2015, 23–31). In such cases a tort claim may serve as much to establish responsibility and to vindicate feelings of outrage and grief as to obtain compensation.

10

The Political Economy
of Compensation Schemes

KI 8: Tort law is not the only game in town

Tort law has its uses. None is unique to tort law. Doing (corrective) justice is distinctive but is shared by contract law, for instance: and as we saw in Chapter 6, some torts are also breaches of contract. Over the past 50 years there have been ongoing public and scholarly debates about alternatives to tort law for performing two of its major uses: compensating for personal injuries and preventing accidents that cause personal injury; compensation and deterrence.

Reviewing the discussion in Chapter 8 will remind you that writers such as Calabresi, Ison and Atiyah found tort law wanting as both a compensation mechanism and a deterrent. Calabresi argued that to be successful as a deterrent, tort law would have to allocate the cost of personal injuries to the 'cheapest cost avoider' rather than on the basis of fault. Tort law's concept of fault, he concluded, did not accurately identify the cheapest cost avoider. Concerning compensation, tort law came in for criticism on several fronts. First, it was argued, tort law's use of fault as the main criterion for entitlement to compensation created an unjustified distinction between people who suffered personal injury as a result of faulty conduct and others who did not and who, therefore, were not entitled to tort compensation, and either had to bear the cost of the injuries themselves or be satisfied with relatively modest social security payments. Second, it was suggested that because of the way the settlement process worked, in a significant proportion of cases the compensation received by the injured person was either too much or too little judged against the rules of tort law about assessment of damages.

In the 1960s and 1970s, a common conclusion was that tort law's shortcomings were so serious that the way forward was not to attempt to reform tort law, however radically, but rather to abolish it as a mechanism for deterring accidents and compensating accident victims, and replace it with more effective tools. On the compensation side, the commonly favoured replacement was some form of social security scheme funded by taxation and calculated according to the needs of the injured. As we saw earlier, in the late 1990s, Atiyah changed his mind about this and favoured a system in which compensation would be funded by private insurance rather than public welfare. On the deterrence side, one idea was a system of 'non-insurable tort fines', penalties that would be imposed, like criminal fines, on the parties best placed to prevent accidents cheaply, and paid into a fund from which harm-sufferers would be compensated.

As we also noted earlier, social-security-type, 'no-fault' compensation schemes funded by taxation were introduced quite widely around the world in the 1970s and 1980s. Most related to road accidents or medical accidents. The most extensive, in New Zealand, covered all accidental injuries. In some cases, the no-fault scheme completely replaced tort law and the tort system in the area of its operation; but in others, the new scheme operated alongside the tort system as a sort of supplement or even competitor. In general, there was little concern that replacing the tort system (at least in the personal-injury accident context) would significantly reduce the incentives for potential harm-doer's to take care because it was accepted on all sides that tort law (backed up by pervasive liability insurance) was an extremely inefficient deterrent. In New Zealand, following the introduction of the accident compensation scheme, some concerns about standards of care in medical treatment were addressed by tightening the legal regulation of the medical profession. On the whole, however, policy-makers and law-makers have not felt the need to take tort law and the tort system seriously as deterrents, to reform them to improve their performance as deterrents, or to provide new deterrents in situations where tort law has been abolished. In the main, they have looked to systems of licensing, regulation and inspection backed up by criminal prosecution to provide the prime tools of safety and accident prevention. This is not to say that tort law is totally useless as a deterrent, and accident prevention is still routinely cited in the scholarly literature and public debates as one of tort law's significant uses. However, policy-makers have treated tort law primarily as a compensation mechanism, and it is in that guise it will be discussed in this chapter.

There are various parameters of the design of 'compensation systems', and we will look at four of these briefly in turn. Notice that in this chapter, the word 'compensation' has a different meaning than in previous chapters. Up until now, it has been used to describe damages for harm inflicted, calculated under the various 'heads' of damages according to the full compensation and cost-of-living principles. Here, 'compensation', as in the term 'compensation system', refers to any monetary payment, however calculated, made on account of harm suffered.

1. FAULT, STRICT LIABILITY AND 'NO-FAULT': TORT AND SOCIAL SECURITY

The main criterion used in tort law to allocate responsibility for personal injuries is fault. Strict liability, regardless of fault, is rare. A shift from fault to strict liability in a compensation scheme increases the size of the pool of potential beneficiaries of the scheme. In theory, too, it reduces the cost of delivering compensation by doing away with the potentially very expensive process of establishing fault. However, both criteria of allocation require proof of a causal connection between the harm-doer's conduct and the harm suffered, which may be very costly to provide.

In a 'no-fault scheme', the nexus between harm-doing and harm-suffering, which is intrinsic to tort law, is broken. It is not necessary, in order to obtain compensation for harm, for claimants to establish a causal connection between the harm and conduct of any individual. Compensation is paid out of a fund, typically financed by some form of taxation. Tax liability may attach to the conduct of some risky activity (as in the case of petrol levies) regardless of whether it causes harm, or to earning income or owning property, for instance. In England, most social security benefits that are triggered by harm-suffering (such as benefits for the sick and disabled) are no-fault in this sense. It follows that the coverage of the social security system of compensation for personal injury is much greater than that of the tort system because the claimant does not have to establish that the harm was caused by the conduct of anyone. It is the harm-suffering as such that attracts compensation, whereas under the tort system, harm-suffering attracts compensation only where it results from the conduct of an identifiable individual.

Because the coverage of the social security system of compensation for personal injuries is wider than that of tort, the two systems overlap. This is important because it takes relatively much longer to process tort claims than social security claims (as a result, for instance, of the need to prove fault and causation in a tort claim), and the harm-sufferer may receive social security benefits to cover living and other costs long before they recover tort damages. Also, of course, harm-sufferers will typically need and receive medical, hospital or nursing care immediately, typically free via the NHS and other publicly-funded services. If the harm-sufferer makes a successful tort claim, the damages assessed will include amounts to cover the costs already covered by social security benefits and the value of publicly-funded care. Such amounts are payable by the harm-doer directly to the government and not to the harm-sufferer. In this way, costs of accidents borne initially by the public purse are ultimately transferred to parties liable in tort and through them, via liability insurance, to a large group of potential harm-doers. To a significant extent, these 'claw-back' arrangements prevent 'double compensation'.

In less serious cases, a combination of social security benefits and NHS services may cover all the harm-sufferer's losses, thus removing any incentive to make a tort claim, even assuming that such a claim would succeed. In more serious, and especially the most serious, cases, the total amount of compensation recoverable in a tort action may greatly exceed the total amount available via social security plus the value of free NHS and social-care services. The more serious the case, the longer it is likely to take to bring the tort-claiming process to a successful conclusion. For this reason, harm-sufferers may be more-or-less dependent for a considerable period on social security benefits and publicly-funded care. This means that even though the cost of social security support and free care will ultimately be transferred to harm-doers, the tort system could not operate as it does without supplementation by the social-security and public-care systems.

In the 'political economy' of personal injury compensation, both the tort system and the social security/care systems play a crucial role. The tort system is particularly important in providing in more serious cases compensation greater than the public system can provide. The public system is particularly important for dealing with many less serious cases and for supporting the more seriously injured pending the completion of the tort process.

2. CAUSE VERSUS HARM: TORT AND THE INDUSTRIAL INJURIES SCHEME

Fault-based and strict-liability compensation regimes (such as tort law) require proof of a causal connection between harm suffered and harm-doing by a responsible individual. No-fault compensation schemes do not. In between are what we might call 'activity-based' compensation schemes. In England, the Industrial Injuries Scheme within the social security system provides an example. In the nineteenth century, in response to great increases in workplace injuries as a result of the Industrial Revolution, tort law developed various rules that made it difficult for employees to recover damages from employers for harm caused in the workplace. The first response to the pro-employer stance of tort law was the introduction, in the late-nineteenth century, of a statutory workers' compensation scheme. This scheme imposed, on employers, liability without fault for workplace injuries. Claimants did not have to prove that the injuries were the result of tortious conduct by the employer, but did have to prove that they arose 'out of and in the course of employment'.

In 1946 workers' compensation was replaced by the Industrial Injuries Scheme (IIS) within the social security system. The IIS was given distinct status within the broader system partly because benefits under the IIS were more generous than other social security benefits. These higher benefits were paid in cases that arose 'out of and in the course of employment'. Whereas workers' compensation had been designed as a substitute for employers' tort liability to overcome its anti-employee bias, by 1946 changes in tort law had redressed the balance; and the question arose of whether the employers' liability tort system should be allowed to operate alongside the IIS. After much debate, the question was resolved positively. Since 1946, the generosity of the IIS relative to non-industrial social security has been whittled away to the point where the relationship between employers' liability tort law and the IIS is similar to that between tort law and social security explored in the previous section.

Another activity-based, publicly-funded compensation scheme is the Criminal Injuries Compensation Scheme (CICS). However, unlike the IIS, the CICS is, in an important sense, a fault-based scheme: claimants must prove that their injuries result from a criminal offence, although they do not have to be able to identify the responsible criminal offender.

The CICS also differs from the IIS in that compensation is assessed according to principles loosely derived from the rules for assessment of tort damages. However, in many cases, CI compensation will be significantly less than compensation calculated according to the tort rules. Unlike employers, however, criminals are rarely worth suing in tort, and so the relationship between the CICS and the tort system is different from that between the social security and tort systems. In certain types of case, criminal courts have jurisdiction to make 'criminal compensation orders' against convicted offenders. These tend to be very small and are set off against compensation recovered under the CICS. For these reasons, the CICS, much more than the IIS, operates as a substitute for or an alternative to the tort system in the area of its operation.

3. LOSS, NEED AND MEANS-TESTING

As we saw in Chapter 7, the concept of compensation in the tort system can be summed up in the 'full compensation' and 'standard-of-living' principles. It focuses, we might say, on what the harm-sufferer has 'lost' by comparing the claimant's position before the harm was suffered with their present, and likely future, position as a result of the tort. Compensation under the CICS is modelled on tort compensation in the sense of focusing on loss inflicted, but is much less generous because it is not 'full' in the tort sense, nor does it aim to maintain the injured person's pre-injury standard of living. Compensation under the IIS has one tort-like element: 'disablement pensions' represent non-pecuniary loss caused by the injuries, and are calculated using a sliding scale of fixed amounts that vary according to the severity of disablement.

Apart from disablement pensions, social security benefits are designed either to replace income or to meet additional costs of disablement. Income-replacement benefits are 'flat-rate'—meaning that they are unrelated to the claimant's pre-injury income—and may be means-tested in favour of the poorest claimants. Benefits to meet additional costs of disablement are generally flat-rate and unrelated to the actual costs incurred by the injured person; they may also be means-tested. One way of describing these basic differences between tort compensation and social security compensation is to say that the former addresses 'loss' whereas the latter addresses 'need'.

4. SOCIAL AND PRIVATE INSURANCE

As we saw in Chapter 7, the tort system of compensation for personal injuries is mainly funded by liability insurance, which spreads the cost of liability amongst a group of potential harm-doers, and is provided by the 'private' insurance market. Another relevant form of insurance protects harm-sufferers from the risk of harm by spreading it amongst a group of potential harm-sufferers. Common examples of 'loss insurance' provided by the private insurance market include life insurance, super-annuation (retirement insurance), travel insurance and health insurance. In the terms we have been using in this chapter, all these types of insurance provide no-fault, cause-based compensation. There are complex rules of tort law, about the interaction between such forms of compensation and the tort system, designed to prevent 'over-compensation' in cases where a harm-sufferer is entitled to both tort compensation and a private-loss-insurance payment.

Loss insurance may also be provided 'publicly'. As originally designed, the funding of the social security system (including the IIS) was primarily based on the insurance principle—entitlement to benefits depended on a person's record of payment of 'national insurance contributions' out of wages. Now, most social security benefits, including those paid under the IIS to workers and ex-workers, are funded by various forms of taxation, not by payment of work-related national insurance contributions.

The sorts of compensation schemes described in this chapter are typically presented in tort books as 'alternatives' to tort. However, since they each have distinctive rules about entitlement to, and assessment and funding of, compensation—in short, because each embodies a different concept of compensation—and because they all differ in these respects from the rules of tort law and tort law's concept of compensation, it is better to think of them as components of a 'political economy' of personal injury compensation systems that interact in various complex ways.

11

The Future of Tort Law

KI 9: Tort law is here to stay—live with it!

In 1970s England there seemed to be a real chance that as a tool of compensation for personal injuries, tort law would be abandoned and replaced with something else. If this had happened, the province of tort law would have shrunk dramatically, chiefly providing protection against interference with property and property-like interests and certain types of investment losses (as happened in New Zealand after the introduction of a broad Accident Compensation Scheme). Today, by contrast, tort law is a firmly entrenched sector of the thriving political economy of personal injury compensation, playing a crucial part, alongside publicly-funded welfare and privately-funded insurance, in dealing with the personal and social disruption caused by death and disablement. And yet all the defects in the system that led reformers 50 years ago to conclude that tort performed both of its main uses (compensation and deterrence) badly, and less well than other available mechanisms, still exist now. Half a century ago, the burning question was how to live without tort law. Now, the important question for those who think that the tort system has serious, endemic and structural flaws, is how to live with it, because it gives no sign of going anywhere anytime soon.

Features of the tort system that have attracted, and continue to attract, most criticism include the following:

— The legal and administrative costs of delivering each £ of tort compensation (30–45 pence) are much higher than those of delivering each £ of social security benefit (10–15 pence). Major reasons for the cost differential are the cost of proving fault and causation, and of assessing damages on an individualised basis (instead of using standardised 'tariffs'). Put differently, the administrative costs of a

> system of liability-with-liability insurance are likely to be relatively much higher than those of a no-fault system funded by taxation, or public or private loss insurance.
> — In tort, the less serious the injuries suffered, the greater the damages recovered tend to be as a proportion of the loss suffered; and conversely, the more serious the injuries, the less the damages as a proportion of the loss suffered. This is mainly because of the way the process of negotiating a settlement typically works, not because the rules of assessment of tort damages require it. By contrast, in theory and in practice, the social security system tends to treat the more seriously disabled relatively more generously than the less seriously disabled.
> — Relative to the injuries suffered, tort damages tend to be, in aggregate, much higher than social security benefits.
> — Relative to social security claims made by the injured and disabled, tort claims probably represent a much smaller proportion of the total number of theoretically possible claims. Put differently, the 'take-up' of social security benefits is probably much higher, relatively, than the take-up of tort damages. This is partly because of the difficulty of proving fault and causation in many cases, especially cases of illness and disease as opposed to traumatic injuries; and partly because of the patchy incidence of compulsory liability insurance.

In assessing such criticisms, it is important to remember that the basic rules and principles of tort law were developed long before the social security system, in its modern form, came into existence. The tort system embodies ideas of individual, interpersonal justice whereas the social security system is based on ideas of social justice. Some people would argue that the value, in terms of interpersonal justice, of a system of liability-with-liability insurance as compared with a no-fault system supported by loss insurance, equals or outweighs its disadvantages and justifies its costs. At the same time, it is worth noting that many who celebrate the 'justice' of the tort system do not oppose the replacement of tort with no-fault. Others argue that the costs of the tort system are acceptable given tort law's value as a deterrent.

However these various arguments are assessed, the current mixed economy of personal injury compensation will probably remain in place for the foreseeable future, with liability and no-fault regimes existing side by side in complex interaction. Even so, it might be worth considering possible changes to tort law that might meet some of the most serious criticisms. So far as causation is concerned, a move from fault-based to strict liability for personal injuries might reduce the cost of proving causation. Under a strict liability regime, causation requires the claimant only to connect harm to a broadly delineated activity and not some narrowly identified act or omission occurring in the course of engaging in the activity. As we have seen, no-fault regimes may also be activity-based and require proof of causation in this sense. Nevertheless, although a no-fault regime may be cause-based, it need not be. By contrast, causation is of the essence of tort law because without it, tort law could not distribute risks and harms in the way it does. A regime that was not cause-based would not be a tort regime.

Because proving fault can be very expensive and time-consuming, a shift to strict liability could also reduce the cost of the tort system. Of course, strict liability distributes risks and losses differently from a fault-based regime. The political question is whether the potential cost savings from such a move would justify changing the standard of liability. This issue has been much discussed over the years, but may deserve further consideration.

Besides causation, another definitional characteristic of tort law and the tort system is that they compensate for losses; but, of course, they share this feature with all 'compensation systems'. Tort compensation differs from compensation as defined in other systems in that it is designed to stabilise people's expectations about how their life will go. It does this by putting the injured person back into the position they were in before they were injured, as far as money can do (let's call this compensation as 'restoration'). De-stabilisation of the financial life-expectations of harm-doers is prevented in most cases by liability insurance. Without pervasive liability insurance, the tort system, as it operates today, would be neither feasible nor (arguably) palatable.

Why should the goal of tort law be to stabilise expectations? After all, this, generally, is not the goal of no-fault compensation systems. Abandonment of the restoration principle does not necessarily reduce the overall costs (made up of the compensation plus the cost of delivery) of a compensation system because any reduction in unit cost may be counter-balanced by an increase in demand—ie in the volume of claims. We have noted that there is reason to think that no-fault systems compensate a greater proportion of eligible claimants than the tort system. If the unit costs of the tort system could be significantly reduced, this might allow the tort system to compensate a greater proportion of potential claimants. There is a (political) trade-off here, of course; but it may be one worth considering if only because the value of the restoration principle is rarely debated, even though it was adopted in the mid-nineteenth century, before the existence of either the welfare state or liability insurance. One down-side (in theory, at least) of abandoning the commitment to restoration might be reduction in tort law's deterrent efficacy.

The restoration principle requires compensation to be assessed in every case according to all the circumstances of that case. This is an important factor in the high cost of the tort system. A move away from the restoration concept might allow less individualisation of compensation and more use of 'tariffs' that group cases into broad categories that can be applied with less detailed fact-finding. This, too, would reduce the administrative cost of the tort system.

This brief discussion raises a host or important, complex and difficult issues (for more see Cane 2007, especially chapter 3); but it is time to stop! We have come a long way from the legal doctrine with which we started, proving to you (I hope) the value of this book's **ORBI** (see page 2): tort law is an authority-based phenomenon that can be, and is best, understood both 'from the inside' as an authoritative source of guidance about how to behave and also 'from the outside', taking into account tort law's character as law, the political and social environments in which tort law operates, tort law's uses, and its competitors.

BIBLIOGRAPHY

Atiyah, PS (1970) *Accidents, Compensation and the Law* (Weidenfield & Nicolson).

Atiyah, PS (1997) *The Damages Lottery* (Hart Publishing).

Barendt, E et al (eds) (1997) *Libel and the Media: The Chilling Effect* (Oxford University Press).

Barker, K, Cane, P, Lunney, M and Trindade, F (2012) *The Law of Torts in Australia* 5th edn (Oxford University Press).

Calabresi, G (1970) *The Costs of Accidents* (Yale University Press).

Cane, P (2003) 'Reforming Tort Law in Australia: A Personal Perspective' 27 *Melbourne University Law Review* 649.

—— (2004) 'The Doctor, the Stork and the Court: A Modern Morality Play' 120 *Law Quarterly Review* 23.

—— (2007) *The Political Economy of Personal Injury Law* (University of Queensland Press).

—— (2013) *Atiyah's Accidents, Compensation and the Law* 8th edn (Cambridge University Press).

Descheemaeker, E (2009) *The Division of Wrongs: A Historical Study* (Oxford University Press).

Galanter, M (1974) 'Why the "Haves" Come out Ahead: Speculations on the Limits of Legal Change' 9 *Law and Society Review* 95.

Gardner, J (2012a) *Law as a Leap of Faith* (Oxford University Press).

—— (2012b) 'Criminals in Uniform' in Duff, RA et al (eds) *The Constitution of Criminal Law* (Oxford University Press).

Giliker, P and Beckwith S (2011) *Tort* 4th edn (Sweet & Maxwell).

Goodin, RE (1989) 'Theories of Compensation' 9 *Oxford Journal of Legal Studies* 56.

—— (1995) *Utilitarianism as a Public Philosophy* (Cambridge University Press).

—— (2010) 'An Epistemic Case for Legal Moralism' 30 *Oxford Journal of Legal Studies* 615.

Hart, HLA (1961) *The Concept of Law* (Clarendon Press).

Honoré, T (1988) 'Responsibility and Luck: The Moral Basis of Strict Liability' 104 *Law Quarterly Review* 530.

—— (1991) 'Are Omissions Culpable?' in Cane, P and Stapleton, J (eds), *Essays for Patrick Atiyah* (Oxford University Press).

—— (1993) 'The Dependence of Morality on Law' 13 *Oxford Journal of Legal Studies* 1.

Ison, T (1967) *The Forensic Lottery* (Staples Press).

Law Commission for England and Wales (1997) *Aggravated, Exemplary and Restitutionary Damages* Law Com No 227.

Linden, A and Feldthusen, B (2015) *Canadian Tort Law* 10th edn (LexisNexis Canada).

McBride, NJ and Bagshaw, R (2015) *Tort Law* 5th edn (Pearson Education).

Mullany, NJ and Handford, PR (2006) *Tort Liability for Psychiatric Damage* 2nd edn (Law Book Company).

Mulheron, R (2016) *Principles of Tort Law* (Cambridge University Press).

Posner, RA (1973) *Economic Analysis of Law* (Little, Brown and Co).

Ripstein, A (2016) *Private Wrongs* (Harvard University Press).

Scanlon, TM (1998) *What We Owe to Each Other* (Harvard University Press).

Sorabji, J (2014) *English Civil Justice after the Woolf and Jackson Reforms* (Cambridge University Press).

Stapleton, J (1986) *Disease and the Compensation Debate* (Oxford University Press).

—— (1994a) *Product Liability* (Butterworths).

—— (1994b) 'In Restraint of Tort' in Birks, P (ed), *Frontiers of Liability* (Oxford University Press).

Stevens, R (2007) *Torts and Rights* (Oxford University Press).

Stone, R (2016) 'Legal Design for the "Good Man"' 102 *Virginia Law Review* 1767.

Varuhas J (2014) 'The Concept of "Vindication" in the Law of Torts: Rights, Interests and Damages' 34 *Oxford Journal of Legal Studies* 253.

Weinrib, EJ (1995) *The Idea of Private Law* (Harvard University Press).

—— (2012a) *The Idea of Private Law* 2nd edn (Oxford University Press).

—— (2012b) *Corrective Justice* (Oxford University Press).

TABLE OF CASES